Brimming with creative inspiration, how-to projects, and useful information to enrich your everyday life, Quarto Knows is a favorite destination for those pursuing their interests and passions. Visit our site and dig deeper with our books into your area of interest: Quarto Creates, Quarto Cooks, Quarto Homes, Quarto Lives, Quarto Drives, Quarto Explores, Quarto Gifts, or Quarto Kids.

© 2018 Quarto Publishing Group USA Inc. Text © 2018 Sam Haynor

First published in 2018 by Young Voyageur Press, an imprint of The Quarto Group, 401 Second Avenue North, Suite 310, Minneapolis, MN 55401 USA. T (612) 344-8100 F (612) 344-8692 www.QuartoKnows.com

Young Voyageur Press titles are also available at discount for retail, wholesale, promotional, and bulk purchase. For details, contact the Special Sales Manager by email at specialsales@quarto.com or by mail at The Quarto Group, Attn: Special Sales Manager, 401 Second Avenue North, Suite 310, Minneapolis, MN 55401 USA.

10 9 8 7 6 5 4 3 2 1

ISBN: 978-0-7603-6101-6

Library of Congress Cataloging-in-Publication Data
Names: Haynor, Sam, 1985- author.
Title: Marvelous makeable monsters : 21 STEAM projects that light up, buzz, launch, and occasionally chomp / Sam Haynor.
Description: Minneapolis, MN : Quarto Publishing Group USA Inc., 2018. | "In this creative project book, STEAM educator Sam Haynor unleashes silly beasts that jump, fly, spin, shake, light up, and even spit. Some creatures are united by their circuits and wires while others are built with more common craft materials. Step by step photos accompany each project. Perfectly safe and fun for younger kids working with adults, most projects can also be tackled by middle-graders with minimal adult help."
Identifiers: LCCN 2018016689 | ISBN 9780760361016 (hc)
Subjects: LCSH: Toy making--Juvenile literature. | Mechanical toys--Juvenile literature. | Squeak toys--Juvenile literature.
Classification: LCC TT174 .H39 2018 | DDC 745.592--dc23
LC record available at https://lccn.loc.gov/2018016689

Acquiring Editor:
Thom O'Hearn

Project Manager:
Alyssa Lochner

Art Director:
James Kegley

Cover & Page Designer:
Evelin Kasikov

Layout:
Diana Boger

Photography:
Jeffery Schwinghammer & Sam Haynor

Illustrations:
Trevor Spencer

Photo Stylist:
Young Xie

Printed in China

MARVELOUS MAKEABLE MONSTERS

21

STEAM Projects That Light Up, Buzz, Launch, and Occasionally Chomp

Sam Haynor

young
voyageur

CONTENTS

INTRODUCTION
OH, HELLO THERE!

Hey, hey, Reddi! Look! Do you see that out there? Is that what I think it is? Oh my, it's a real-life human! Wow, gee, sorry to stare. I mean, we heard stories about you humans when we were kids, but I thought that was all just make-believe! You even have five-fingered tentacles and twice as many eyes as a cyclops, just like in the stories. Wowowowowowow!

Well, human friend, you arrived just in time. I'm Yullo, and this here's Reddi, and we're just getting ready to go on an adventure. The problem is that a lot of the marvelous monsters we're going to see have to be made first. Oh, right! Silly me, I forgot that you humans are "born" and all, right? Sounds weird. Here in monster kingdom, we're all *made*. That's right, like put together with glue and stuff. We would make these monsters ourselves, but, well, we're tiny. You'll help us, won't you, giant human friend? Yes? Sounds great! We better get you set up with tools and everything, and you can even practice by making us! Just make me a little bigger than Reddi, okay?

Okay, ready? Let's GO!

KNOW YOUR TOOLS
YOUR MONSTER WORKSHOP

Keep these tools close, and you'll be able to go far!

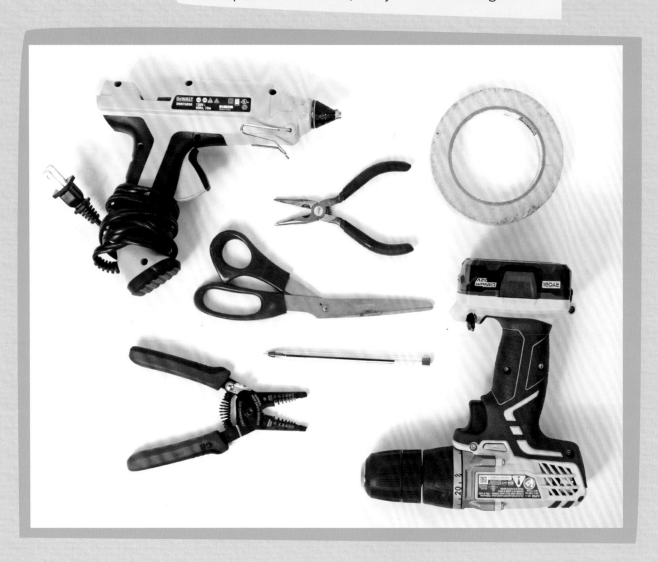

Since you're about to go on an adventure, you're probably wondering what to pack. We bet you have burning questions like, "How many sandwiches should I bring?" and "Just how many humans *have* escaped from the Caves of Maybe No Return?" Great questions! And, well, as this is an adventure, we don't have *all* the answers. We'd say to start by packing some imagination and checking out these monster-making basics.

HOT GLUE GUN

FOR STICKING THINGS TOGETHER. This is like the magician's wand of monster making. Anything's possible when you have hot glue. To use a hot glue gun, you'll also need hot glue sticks that go with it. These look like plastic versions of string cheese and they come in tubes that fit in the hole in the back of your glue gun. When you plug the hot glue gun in, it heats up and melts your glue sticks into liquid glue. Pull the trigger, and out comes hot goo that then cools and can glue all sorts of stuff together. Try it out! Be careful with your fingers, though. Both the glue gun and the glue itself get hot and they can cause burns if you touch them. Practice, be careful, and you'll find this a great tool.

SCISSORS AND PLIERS

FOR CUTTING, SNIPPING, AND BENDING. Scissors probably aren't big news to you, but they're still spectacular for cutting all sorts of materials. Pliers are like the strong robot fingers you always wished you had. With pliers in hand, you can pinch and bend thick wire this way and that. If you look closely at your pliers, you'll see that in addition to bending wire, their tips also can *cut* wire. This makes them perfect to cut thick wire to make arms, legs, and antennae for your monsters.

PENS, PENCILS, AND MARKERS

FOR SKETCHING AND DECORATING. All monsters are beautiful on the inside, but with pens and markers you can make them beautiful on the outside too. For more on decorating, see page 13.

WIRE STRIPPERS

FOR ELECTRONICS WIRING. For any electronics, wire strippers will be your best friend. They look kind of like pliers, but with swiss cheese–like holes that show up when they're closed. You can place wire in the matching-sized hole, grip it, and pull away the plastic coating surrounding the metal of your wire. This makes your electronics ready to connect! Just like the pliers, the wire strippers also have a way to grip at the end and cut toward the middle. Grab some wire and play around!

TAPE

FOR KEEPING IT ALL TOGETHER. There isn't just one way to stick things together. Masking tape, scotch tape, duct tape, and even copper tape (for making circuits) will all be part of this adventure, so get used to them! Try tearing, cutting, and sticking several kinds tapes to different materials to see what works best in various situations.

FINDING STUFF

Motors, battery packs, cell batteries, buzzers, LEDs, wire and magnet wire, and more can all be found at electronics stores. Copper tape and springs can be found at the hardware store. Most of the rest can be found at a variety of stores. When in doubt, look online!

SAFETY THINGS

In addition to monster bites, there are a few other things that might hurt if you use them incorrectly. Be careful with tools like hot glue guns and always let your adult helper decide what to do for the projects with powerful tools like drills or dangerous materials like dry ice. Projects that need you to be a little extra careful will have this symbol ❗ next to them to give you a heads-up. You can always bring an adult helper in to assist on other projects as well. They'll have fun!

STEAM STUFF

As you make the monsters in this book, you'll see the word "STEAM" here and there. Now, you might be familiar with "steam," which has to do with water and energy. But this is a different type of STEAM. It stands for: Science, Technology, Engineering, Art, and Math. Don't let those words scare you off. STEAM is fun! It's all about making stuff and figuring out how what we create relates to other things in the world. When you wire up the Wobbling Wandersnatch, send a High-Flying Heliflopper skyward, or add fashionable buttons to Fortoona the Truthteller, that's STEAM!

HOOKING UP ELECTRONICS

Some monsters need electricity to come alive. With these monsters, you will be making circuits with a battery and some neat electronics parts. You'll be hooking up motors and buzzers using metal wire to connect them. Most metal wire you find will be coated with plastic. Use wire strippers to remove the plastic from the wire ends so you can join them together to make the circuit come to life! The electronics can sometimes be tricky, so take time to test things out. Aluminum foil wrapped around connections can help electricity flow, and hot glue or tape can help the wires stick together. Don't worry too much: the projects will all have helpful photos.

USE WHAT YOU HAVE

It's okay if you don't have all the materials in the instructions. You can often substitute things you have around the house for things you don't have. Don't have craft cubes for feet? Glue on some beads! Don't have beads? Glue on some pompoms! Experiment with where you can substitute other materials and where you can't. After all, that's how inventions are made.

SNAP A PHOTO!

Your creations deserve to be remembered. You can take pictures of the monsters in their worlds, draw them, or even just write about what you did. Keeping a Monster Journal with entries for each project can be a great way to keep track of all the marvels you've created.

KEEP TRYING

Some steps can be hard at first, especially the ones marked ❗. But don't give up, because getting those steps right might mean learning something new. If you feel yourself get really stuck, look at the photos again or ask a friend for help. Two minds are better than one!

DECORATE YOUR OWN WAY

You don't have to make monsters **exactly** like they are here. In fact, it's better if they're different and your own. Add your style with craft materials and markers to make these monsters fabulous and unique. Here are some great supplies to throw into a craft box that can be used for just about every monster.

- Pompoms
- Googly eyes
- Pipe cleaners
- Craft foam
- Markers
- Craft beads
- Straws
- Craft sticks

EXPERIMENT!

Not only can you customize the way the monsters look, but you can change how they act too! One of the wobbling monsters can change how deeply it wobbles and how high it jumps depending on where you put the cork. Another balancing monster changes the way it leans when you adjust its weights. Experiment to see what changing some part of your monster does to the way it acts. Can your monster wiggle faster? Launch higher? Extend farther? After you make a monster, there's so much you can change to make it even more marvelous! Try out your ideas and see what works best.

MAKING REDDI AND YULLO

Let's see here, Reddi. You packed the pompoms and the paper clips. I got the peanut butter sandwiches, and we're both grabbing some extra batteries. What else do we need on our adventure? Oh, right, us! We're pretty simple to bring to life, human friend, and we're not too ticklish or anything. And would you look at that: we even light up!

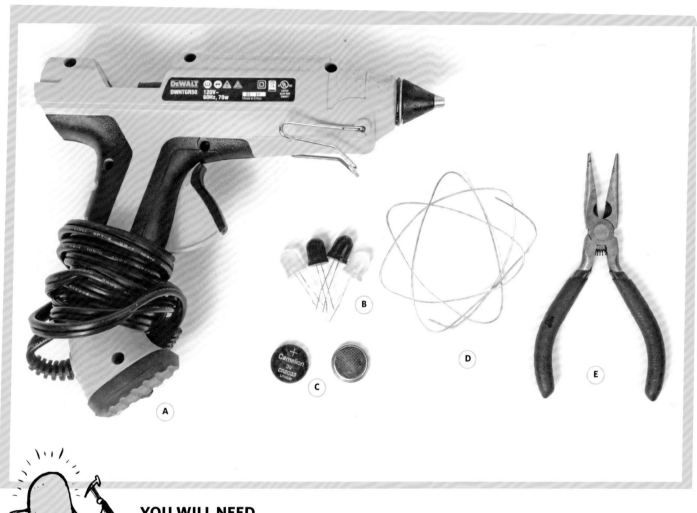

YOU WILL NEED

Ⓐ Glue gun   Ⓑ 2 big LEDs (1 yellow and 1 red)   Ⓒ 3-volt button cell battery

Ⓓ 12 inches thick steel wire   Ⓔ Pliers

MAKE YOUR MONSTER

1. **CUT AND BEND LED LEGS.** Use pliers to cut the legs to the same length, and then bend them to make feet.

2. **BEND WIRE ARMS.** Cut a short piece of wire and curl both ends to make arms with hands.

4. **LET IT GLOW.** Hold legs against both sides of your battery, and watch the LED light up! Flip the battery if the LED doesn't light up the first time.

3. **GLUE ARMS AROUND WAIST.** Bend arms around LED and dab with hot glue.

5. **MAKE LOTS OF FRIENDS!** Reddi and Yullo come from big families, after all. Make a whole crew!

STEAM STUFF

BRIGHT LIGHTS

Reddi and Yullo are kind, but a little light in the head. Or rather, they have a little light for a head. When you touch their legs to either side of the battery, you are completing a circuit that lights them up. The electricity passes from one side of the battery, through one leg, through a channel in the head, through the other leg, and back through the battery. As the electricity passes through the head, it lights up. Electricity has to pass through an LED the right way to make it light up. If your LED isn't lighting, just try flipping the battery around.

EXPLORE SOME MORE

Reddi and Yullo are explorers. You can make tools for them to hold, scenes for them to be in, or even entire worlds. Try making a scene and photographing it from their perspective. What are some objects that are small to you that might be huge to Reddi and Yullo?

1
THE CASTLE OF CLOUDS

Sorry we're a little late! We just got back from doing laps around one of our moons, and well, I don't even know where Yullo is. *Yulloooooo!* Hmm, I swear she was just behind me when we entered the atmosphere. Oh well, she'll catch up. Wow, you can really see for miles up here. Hey, look, there are some monsters over there!

You'll soon meet the hungry and oh-so-stretchy **Extendo Dragon** (page 28)! And you can already see the flock of **Dizzyheaded Dodons** (page 32) circling around and around over by their nests. Of course, the **High-Flying Helifloppers** (page 25) are some of our favorites, since they let us hitch free rides. And look over there! It's the highest mountaintop in monster kingdom and the **Balancing Bodunk** (page 20) is sitting on top of it. Yullo might be down there already, so we better check it out.

THE BALANCING BODUNK

You're pretty lucky there, human friend. This isn't just *a* Bodunk. It's *the* Bodunk. In fact, they say this Balancing Bodunk keeps the *whole planet* in balance. That's right. One time, when we were little, the Bodunk slipped. Monsters started flying off the face of the planet left and right. Monster school was cancelled for three years! It was pretty cool. So go on, give it a nudge.

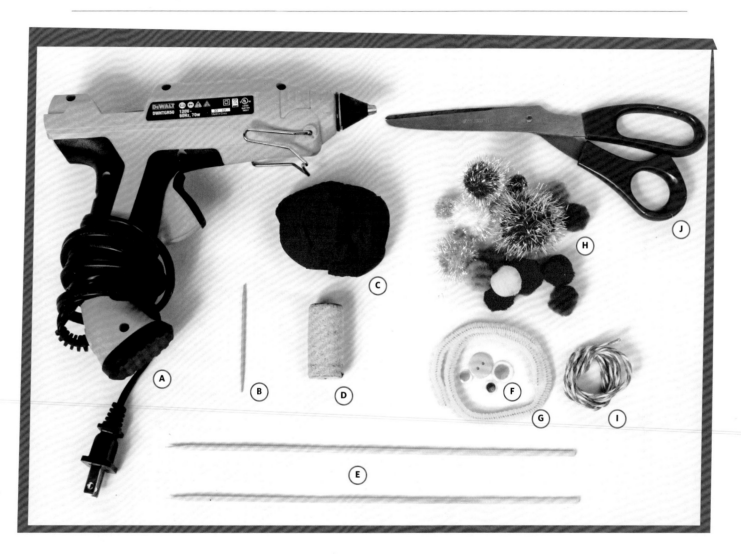

YOU WILL NEED

Ⓐ Glue gun   Ⓑ 1 toothpick   Ⓒ 2 balls of clay (ping-pong–size)   Ⓓ 1 cork   Ⓔ 2 skinny wood skewers

Ⓕ 1 googly eye   Ⓖ 1 pipe cleaner   Ⓘ Small amount of yarn (optional)   Ⓗ Pompoms   Ⓙ Scissors

1. **DECORATE YOUR CORK.** Glue on some pompom hair, add a big googly eye right in the middle of its face. Make a nice yarn sweater, and give it some pipe cleaner arms. Deck it out!

2. **STICK TOOTHPICK IN BOTTOM OF CORK.** A shorter toothpick will be more stable, but a longer one will make the balancing act more spectacular.

3. **POKE WOOD SKEWERS IN SIDES OF CORK.** Make sure both skewers are angled downward, like in the photo.

4. **FORM BALLS OF CLAY ON SKEWER ENDS.** Make them approximately the same size.

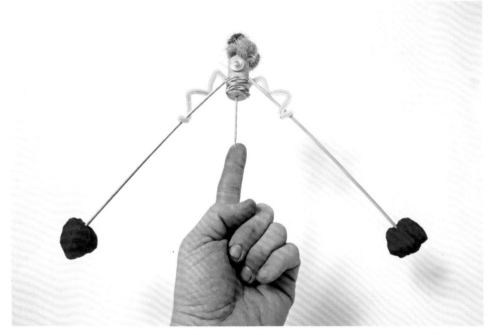

5. **GET THE BODUNK BALANCING!** Stick it on aynthing! Give it a twirl! Just *try* to knock that Bodunk over. It's just not that easy.

STEAM STUFF

KEEPING BALANCE

What keeps a Bodunk upright, and why doesn't it fall? It all has to do with its *center of mass*. You can find the center of mass by trying to figure out where it balances best. If you take a ruler for example, slide your finger under it until it balances. You found the center of mass! For people, the center of our mass is somewhere between our bellies and our hips. That's our balancing point, and if we lean it to far beyond our feet, we fall down. With the Bodunk, however, the heavy clay balls add a lot of weight below its toothpick foot. The Bodunk's center of mass is actually below the toothpick. This makes it very stable. It tries to stand up even when you knock it over. See if you can change its center of mass by changing where the balls of clay are. What happens?

TRY IT!

Want to try to make a Bodunk that's off-balance? It's not as easy as you might think. Try changing the toothpick length, the angle of the wood skewers in the sides of the cork, and even the amount of clay on each side. When you change these things, how does the Bodunk's balance change? When doesn't it balance at all?

HIGH-FLYING HELIFLOPPERS

You really haven't flown until you've *flopped*. The High-Flying Helifloppers are like a rocket ship mixed with a bag of glitter. Needless to say, we're frequent flyers. You can send us up flying in one and we'll twirl back to the ground like a feather. Just pull back and watch us soar! We'd make you one, but we mentioned we're tiny, right?

FAST FACTS

WHAT: a finger flinger that shoots into the sky and spins gracefully on the way down

STEAM STUFF: air resistance ▪ **ROOM TO TWIRL:** Helifloppers are born for the sky, so make sure they have plenty of room to fly. Go outside and find a clear space free of obstacles overhead. Pull back, release, and watch them soar. ▪ **DIFFICULTY:** ★ ▪ **COST:** $

YOU WILL NEED

(A) Glue gun (B) 1 rubber band (C) Transparent tape (D) Scissors (E) 1 googly eye (F) 1 pipe cleaner

(G) 1 paper clip (H) 1 notecard or piece of cardstock (I) 1 wide straw (J) Tinsel (optional) ● Marker

MAKE YOUR MONSTER

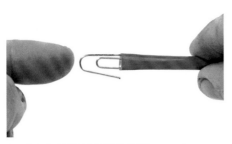

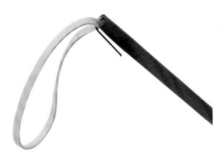

1. **GLUE PAPER CLIP IN STRAW.** Leave the end of the paper clip sticking out the end of the straw as a hook.

2. **SLIDE RUBBER BAND ONTO PAPER CLIP.**

3. **PLACE TINSEL ON TAPE.** This is optional, but makes your Heliflopper look stylish while flying.

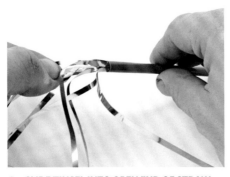

4. **SLIDE TINSEL INTO OPEN END OF STRAW.** Fold the tape up and push it in the straw's open end. The bunched up tape will keep it snug against the straw walls.

5. **CUT NOTECARD SO IT HAS 3 FINGERS.** Make 2 cuts, each going about halfway down the card.

6. **TAPE NOTECARD AROUND STRAW END AND FOLD.** ❗ After you tape it around the base, experiment with folding down the 3 fingers of the cardstock to make a propeller. To begin, try folding each finger of paper so that they are angled in the same direction. When it flies, this design will send the Heliflopper into a gentle spin. You can experiment with other designs later too!

7. **ADD PERSONALITY.** Glue on a face with googly eyes and a pipe cleaner, and draw on a body with a marker.

8. **FLING IT!** Pull it back, and let your Heliflopper soar! It may take some practice to get the flinging, and it may take some adjustments to make it go really high. Shoot for the stars!

STEAM STUFF
AIR RESISTANCE

When your Heliflopper falls from the sky, it might be falling with a twirl. When an object moves quickly through air, air pushes back against it. It's just like when you're biking really fast, and all of a sudden, you feel wind even when there wasn't any previously. When the Heliflopper falls, it is running into air that is pushing up on it. If all the propellers are slightly angled the same direction, every little bit of air that bounces off them one way sends the Heliflopper twirling in the other. It falls through the air like a propeller. What other things have you seen that demonstrate air resistance?

EXPLORE SOME MORE

The airplane wasn't invented overnight, and neither was the perfect Heliflopper. Try making others, and experiment with the design to make it fly better. What if you use a smaller notecard, or give it four propeller blades instead of three? What about a shorter straw or one with more weight in the front? How do the Helifloppers fly differently?

EXTENDO DRAGON

Whatever you do, do *not* tell our mom we showed you how to make Extendo Dragons. They stopped by last month and ate all of her trees. And her car. In fact, we've seen them eat just about everything. The tricky thing is they're just so *stretchy*. You think you put something out of their reach, and then they just extend across the room and chomp it up. Just stay near their feet, and you can send them extending to grab stuff for you too!

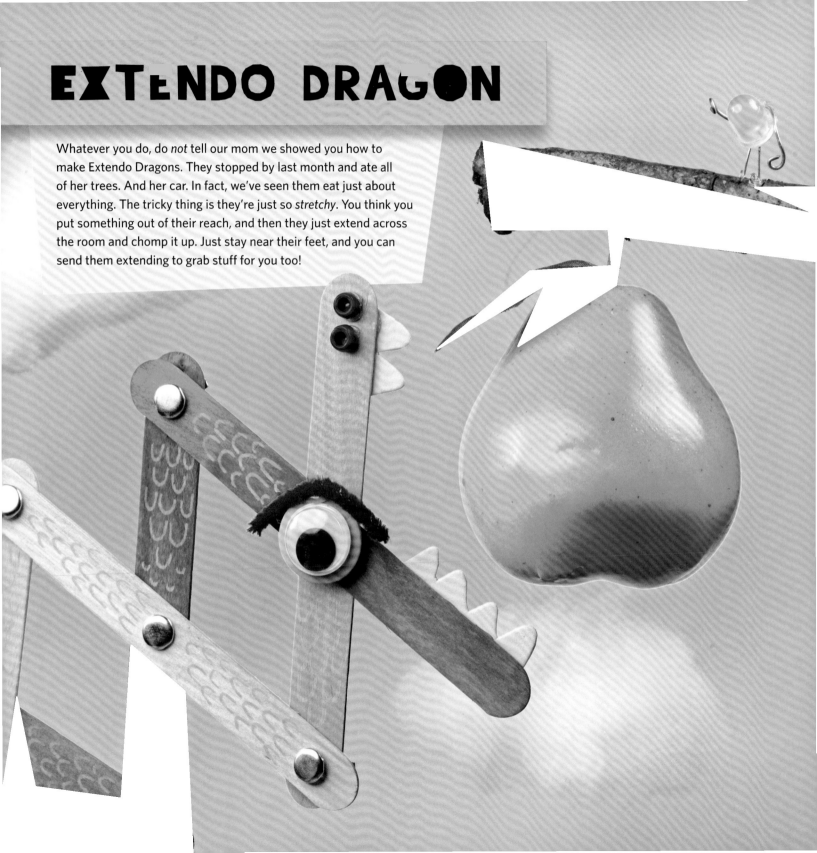

WHAT: a mechanical monster that extends like a scissor lift ▪ **DRILL TIME:** You'll need an adult helper with a drill to make holes to connect your Extendo Dragon together. See page 30 for more on drilling. **STEAM STUFF:** Levers ▪ **DIFFICULTY:** ★ ★ ▪ **COST:** $

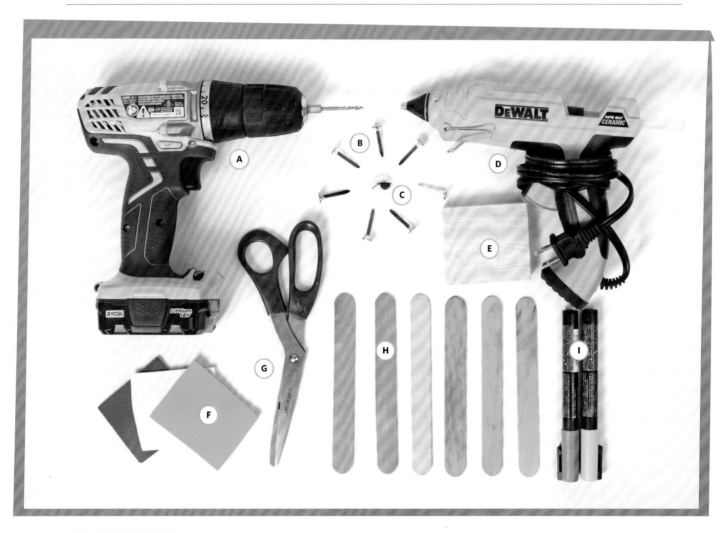

YOU WILL NEED

Ⓐ Drill (with small bit), and an adult helper to use it Ⓑ 7 metal brad fasteners Ⓒ Googly eyes Ⓓ Glue gun
Ⓔ Wood block for drilling Ⓕ Scraps of craft foam Ⓖ Scissors Ⓗ 6 large craft sicks Ⓘ Markers

IT'S TIME TO DRILL!

Drills are great for making circular holes in things. But because they can be dangerous, your adult helper should be deciding whether they use the drill or whether you're ready to try. If you get to drill a hole, you'll want to know a couple things first. To make holes, you'll need *bits*, which are the long things that you screw into the end of drills. It's best to have a set with a couple of different sizes of bits. It's also great to have a surface that you can drill on that's okay to scratch up, because once you drill the hole you mean to drill, you don't want to accidentally drill a hole into your table. A scrap piece of wood works really well, and you can use it over and over again. When you drill, make sure to pay close attention. Use both hands, but keep your fingers away from the drilling.

1. **DRILL HOLES IN CRAFT STICKS.** ❗ Stack them up and have your adult helper drill 3 holes through all the sticks. Your helper should drill really slowly, making 1 hole near each end and 1 in the middle.

2. **USE BRAD TO CONNECT MIDDLE HOLES OF 2 CRAFT STICKS.** Put 2 craft sticks together to make an X and push a brad through both center holes. Flatten out the brad's legs to keep the craft sticks connected.

3. **CONNECT MORE CRAFT STICKS.** Use the pattern in the photo to connect more craft sticks. You can use 6 to start, but why not keep going to make your dragon extend even farther?

4. **ADD A DRAGON FACE.** All good dragons have a little bite to them. Cut and glue on some teeth from foam, add some eyes, and add any other features you think your dragon needs.

5. **DRAW ON SCALES.** A dragon always appreciates a little skin texture.

6. **EXTENDO THAT DRAGON!** Push together the 2 craft sticks farthest from the dragon's face, and watch it extend and bite!

STEAM STUFF

LEVERS

You may not realize it, but you just built a machine. A machine is simply something that, when you do something to it, it does something different in response. When you squeeze the two craft sticks at the end of the Extendo Dragon together, the dragon responds by extending. Each of these craft sticks is an example of a *lever*, a simple machine that's a long bar attached to other things. When these levers work together, they can extend and fold together. The extending motion is something used a lot in the real world. An easy place to find an example of this is a *scissors lift*. That's a kind of construction machine used to raise people or things high in the air. See if you can find one!

EXPLORE SOME MORE

Time to add some other dragons to the castle. You can probably tell that there's no limit to how long an Extendo Dragon can be. What would happen if you added more craft sticks? Try adding more on, and once you've tried that, try drilling holes in different places on the craft sticks. You'll find that you can make all sorts of strange Extendo creatures.

IZZY EAR ED DODONS

These birds may be pretty, but they just can't seem to keep their heads on straight. Yep, those heads just keep on spinning. Oh look, it seems like they have some eggs that are about to hatch! If you think the adults are wacky, you should see the babies. They're like a cross between a merry-go-round and a blender.

WHAT: long-necked straw birds whose heads spin with a puff of air
STEAM STUFF: opposing forces ▪ **DIFFICULTY:** ★ ★ ▪ **COST:** $

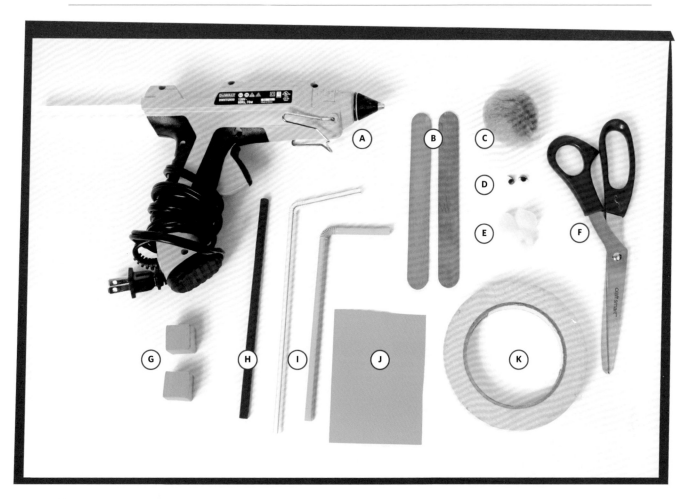

YOU WILL NEED

Ⓐ Glue gun Ⓑ 2 craft sticks Ⓒ Pompoms Ⓓ Googly eyes Ⓔ Beads (for feet) Ⓕ Scissors

Ⓖ 2 craft blocks or beads (for feet) Ⓗ 1 straight straw (different width than bendy straws)

Ⓘ 2 bendy straws Ⓙ Colored paper scraps Ⓚ Masking tape ● Ball of yarn (optional)

1. **TAPE END OF BENDY STRAW AND SNIP THE CORNER.** 🛈 Tape the short end of the bendy straw closed, and cut off a corner like in the photo. Bend it down so that the open corner is pointing to the side. Now snip the long end of the straw down to about half its size. This straw will be the head.

2. **FIT THE 3 STRAWS TOGETHER.** Now that you have your head straw, let's add a straight body straw and a bendy trail straw. Glue the bendy (tail) straw into the body straw, but leave head straw loose so it can move freely. Make sure it can slide either on the outside or the inside of the body straw easily.

3. **GLUE ON CRAFT STICK LEGS.** Glue craft sticks onto either side of where the body and tail straws meet. These are the Dodon's legs. Glue the craft blocks or beads onto the end of the legs as feet.

4. **MAKE A FACE.** On top of the taped bendy straw, add some pompoms, a paper beak, and some eyes to bring your Dodon to life.

5. **WRAP THE BODY IN YARN.** Every Dodon needs to stay warm. Decorate yours with yarn to give it a sweater.

6. **BLOW IN TAIL TO MAKE DODON SPIN!** As you blow into the tail, the head of the Dodon should rise and start to spin around. If it doesn't, check to make sure that it can move freely and that the corner you snipped is facing to the side. Let's get dizzy!

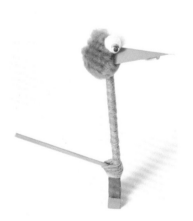

STEAM STUFF

OPPOSITE FORCES

Dodons like to stay on alert, but they need your help to do so. When you blow into a Dodon's tail, that air goes through the body, into the head, and out the side of the Dodon beak. See if you can trace the direction that the air is moving all the way through. When air escapes out the side, it pushes the straw the opposite way, making your Dodon all dizzyheaded. It works just like when you let go of a balloon. Air comes out of the balloon's neck, and as it does, the balloon rockets in the opposite direction. When something is pushed in different directions, those pushes are called *opposing forces*. Opposing forces are behind everything from swimming to launching rockets into space to making a Dodon's head twirl.

TRY IT!

Try making your Dodon another head. What happens if you switch which side of the straw the cut corner is on?
What happens if you make the hole bigger or smaller, or make it further up the straw?

2

THE BEASTLY BIG TOP

WHOA THERE! GOOD HORSEY!

Under this tent you will see mysterious creatures from far and wide to dazzle and delight. You'll find impossible beasts and wondrous whatsits all the way from—*naw, we're just kidding*! These are a bunch of our old friends we invited to put on a show. We knew the **Tossing Tooboks** (page 42) when they were just launching lint balls. The **A-maze-ing Chompi** (page 46) used to be our school mascot. We were in the same class with the **Wobbling Wandersnatch** (page 50) and it could never sit still. Oh look! **Cycloptoglovus** (page 38) is warming up for the first act! Grab some popcorn and let's enjoy the show.

CYCLOPTOGLOVUS

From a one-eyed 360 to a no-look, four-fingered Cycloptoflip: is there anything this creature can't do?! You're pretty lucky to see this, human friend. Cyclo is a monster kingdom legend. One time, in the Monster Olympics, Cyclo jumped around a lightning bolt, through a tornado, and over a pit of lava. And that was just in warm-ups. When you make Cycloptoglovus, you should teach it some new cool tricks from your world!

FAST FACTS

STEAM STUFF: craft and design ■ **DIFFICULTY:** ★ ■ **COST:** 💲💲 ■ **MOTTO:** "I'm gloving it!"

Ⓐ Glue gun   Ⓑ 1 Styrofoam ball   Ⓒ Scraps of craft foam and felt   Ⓓ 1 colorful glove*   Ⓔ Pompoms

Ⓖ Scissors   Ⓗ Ball of yarn (optional)   Ⓕ Pipe cleaners   ⬤ Wood block (optional)

*This project uses a glove, which can be a great craft item. Make sure you use a glove you have permission to craft with, so you don't annoy your family *too* much.

MAKE YOUR MONSTER

1. **STUFF THE FEET.** Tuck in the thumb of the glove. Next, stuff 1 pompom in each of the middle 2 fingers of the glove and shove the pompom to the fingertip.

2. **MAKE SOME SHOES.** Use some yarn or pompoms to make some fly footwear.

3. **GLUE ON SOME HANDS.** Cut some foam hands and glue them to the ends of the outer 2 fingers of the glove.

OPTIONAL

4. **INSERT WOOD BLOCK INTO GLOVE (OPTIONAL).** This can help with gluing for the next step, since it stretches out your glove and keeps the sides of the glove from sticking together.

5. **GIVE IT A FACE!** Cut the Styrofoam ball in half, and glue half on as an eye. Decorate the face with pompoms, felt, and pipe cleaners.

6. **TAKE YOUR CYCLOPTOGLOVUS OUT ON THE TOWN!** Tuck in your thumb and slide your other fingers into the arms and legs of your Cycloptoglovus puppet. Take it for a stroll! What poses can you do? You can give it a skateboard, surfboard, magic carpet, or anything else you like to cruise around on.

EXPLORE SOME MORE

A Cycloptoglovus can get lonely all by itself, so why not make it some friends? After all, gloves come in pairs, right? Try out a different design and see what other personalities you can bring out. See what poses you can make. Can you make your Cycloptoglovuses clap? Walk? Run? Break dance? Play the guitar? If you have any miniature toys, let your Cycloptoglovus at them!

TOSSING TOOBOK

Step right up! Pull back on the Toobok and hit the target with a pompom to win a prize! You can win amazing prizes like, well . . . more pompoms! What more could you want, anyway? If you accidentally hit a Toobok, though, it's not a pretty sight. They get all snarly and drooly and stuff. So, uh, aim well?

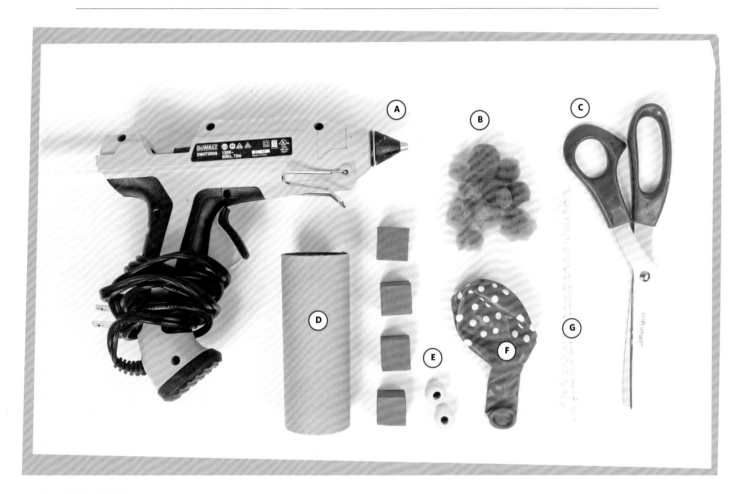

YOU WILL NEED

Ⓐ Glue gun   Ⓑ Pompoms, beads, googly eyes, and other craft supplies   Ⓒ Scissors   Ⓓ 1 small cardboard tube

Ⓔ 4 cubes or beads (for feet)   Ⓕ 1 small balloon   Ⓖ Pipe cleaners

1. **CUT OFF THE SKINNY PART OF THE BALLOON'S MOUTH.** Try to cut it just where it begins widening. We'll be using the wide part in the next step.

2. **STRETCH THE BALLOON OVER THE TUBE'S END.** Pull it tight like a drum.

3. **GLUE ON 4 FEET.** Use 4 cubes, beads, or anything similar to make a stable base. Glue them near the open end of the tube, so the Toobok leans back onto its balloon-covered end.

4. **MAKE A FACE!** Add pompoms, beads, googly eyes, pipe cleaners, or anything else to the open end of the tube to gve your Toobok some character. Just don't cover up the opening too much. Pompoms will be flying out of there.

5. **FEED THE TOOBOK POMPOMS.** You can try 1 at a time or more. Tooboks have quite the appetite.

6. **SPIT SOME POMPOMS!** Pull back the balloon behind, letting pompoms roll down into the balloon. The balloon will grip the cardboard tube pretty well, but you can help secure it with your other hand too. Release the balloon to launch your pompoms at a target! And then do it all over again.

TRY IT!

Try making a target! A small container such as a cup works well, or even a target with the stiff side of Velcro attached to it. Try to launch from different angles and with different numbers of pompoms to see how the flight and accuracy is affected. How far can you fling a pompom with a Toobok?

Hold on to your wallet. These Chompis have a thing for eating pennies. Then again, the pennies always come back out the other end a couple seconds later, so it's not so bad. Some even say the pennies are shinier coming out than when they go in, but I don't like to think about it. Go ahead and give it a try. No, not eating pennies, human friend. I mean build a Chompi and try feeding it. I'll go grab the broom.

FAST FACTS

WHAT: a standing cardboard creature with a blind maze for coins inside
STEAM STUFF: puzzles ■ **DIFFICULTY:** ★ ★ ■ **COST:** ⑤

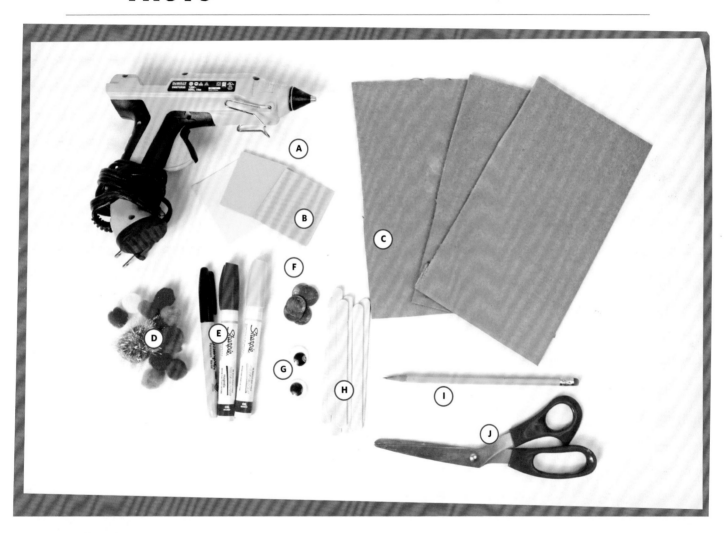

YOU WILL NEED

Ⓐ Glue gun   Ⓑ Scraps of craft foam   Ⓒ 3 large pieces of cardboard   Ⓓ Pompoms   Ⓔ Markers   Ⓕ Small coin

Ⓖ 2 googly eyes   Ⓗ Several thin craft sticks   Ⓘ Pencil   Ⓙ Scissors   ● yarn (optional)

1. **DRAW CHOMPI ON CARDBOARD.** Pencil your monster outline large enough to have a maze inside.

2. **CUT OUT 2 CHOMPIS.** Cut out 2 identical versions of the same outline.

3. **DRAW A MAZE ON 1 OF THE PIECES.** ❗ Make Chompi's mouth the start and finish at Chompi's rear. Draw the walls of the maze far enough apart so your coin can fit between them. Use your coin to measure the space as you draw.

4. **MAKE CRAFT STICK WALLS.** Cut craft sticks as needed and glue their edges to the maze walls you've drawn. Keep checking to make sure the sticks are far enough apart for the coin to fit between them.

5. **GLUE 2 CARDBOARD PIECES TOGETHER.** Apply glue to the other edges of the craft sticks, and then position the second piece of cardboard onto these glued edges.

6. **ADD CARDBOARD FEET.** Cut out feet out of the third piece of cardboard. Glue them onto Chompi to make supports, so Chompi can stand on its own.

7. **MAKE CHOMPI GLAMOROUS.** Give Chompi some eyes, hair, skin coloring, arms, or any other features you like. (But of course with Chompi, it's what's on the inside that counts.)

OPTIONAL

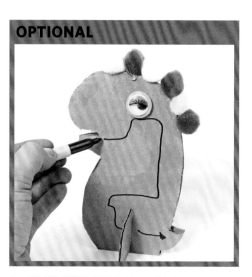

8. **DRAW MAZE GUIDE ON BACK.** If you want to help other people out, draw a maze key on the back side of Chompi.

9. **WHO CAN SOLVE THE A-MAZE-ING CHOMPI?** Put a coin in Chompi's mouth, and have people rotate Chompi to see if they can get the coin to come out its behind.

EXPLORE SOME MORE

There is always another puzzle to solve. After you've made one Chompi, try making other more complex mazes by making larger and more detailed Chompis. In larger versions, you can add elements such as multiple paths.

TRY IT!

Time yourself and others trying to get a coin through the maze. Can you figure it out by feeling alone? Are you faster when you know the path? What about trying it with your eyes closed?

WOBBLING WANDERSNATCH

Nice horsey. Niiiiiiice horsey. The Wobbling Wandersnatch may be the main event, but it has the nerves of a hamster that's had seven cups of soda. I'll just slooooowly approach, feed it this battery, and . . . here we go! It jumps! It bucks! It wobbles and wiggles! It's completely out of control!

WHAT: a motorized creature whose off-balance tail makes it jump, wiggle, and scoot

STEAM STUFF: symmetry ∎ **DIFFICULTY:** ★ ★ ★ ∎ **COST:** $ $ $

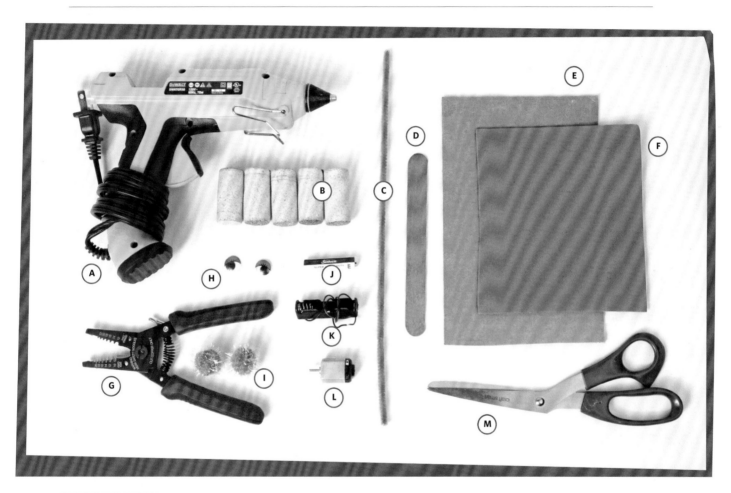

YOU WILL NEED

Ⓐ Glue gun   Ⓑ 5 corks (or other items for legs)   Ⓒ Pipe cleaners   Ⓓ 1 wide craft stick   Ⓔ Medium-size piece of cardboard   Ⓕ Medium-size piece of craft foam   Ⓖ Wire stripper   Ⓗ 2 googly eyes   Ⓘ A few pompoms   Ⓙ 1 AAA battery   Ⓚ 1 AAA battery pack   Ⓛ 1 3-volt DC motor   Ⓜ Scissors

1. **CUT OUT CARDBOARD AND FOAM BASE.** Choose a shape that's wide enough to fit the electronics, and then cut the same shape out of both materials.

2. **GLUE CARDBOARD AND FOAM TOGETHER.**

3. **ATTACH 4 CORK FEET.** Glue 1 end of each cork to the cardboard.

4. **GLUE THE MOTOR ONTO FOAM.** Make sure the spinning part of the motor is hanging off the back of the base.

5. **ATTACH AND GLUE BATTERY PACK.** Attach 1 wire to each of the 2 metal tabs on the motor. If needed, use the wire stripper to cut and expose the wire from its plastic covering. When in place, glue the battery pack to the foam base.

6. **SLIDE ON CORK TAIL.** Push the remaining cork onto the motor spindle so the cork is off-center. You can adjust and experiment with this later.

7. **GIVE YOUR WANDERSNATCH A FACE.** Make the face as majestic as silly as you like. A craft stick cut in 2 pieces make great antennae to which you can attach pompoms and googly eyes. Pipe cleaners are perfect for arms.

8. **RELEASE THE WANDERSNATCH!** Slide a battery into the battery pack, and watch the Wandersnatch spring to life!

STEAM STUFF

BALANCED SIDES

When something is the same on one side as it is on the other, we call it *symmetrical*. Many parts of machines have symmetry. The Wandersnatch's motor, for example, is symmetrical in a couple of ways. What isn't symmetrical about the Wandersnatch is the tail. With more cork on one side of the motor than on the other, the difference in weight makes the Wandersnatch shaky. Sometimes not having symmetry can be useful in machines, and it's a neat thing to look out for. Take a look around, and see where you can find symmetry or a lack of it.

TRY IT!

You can see that the tail wags the Wandersnatch. Try taking the tail off the motor and sticking the spindle into a different part of the cork. See how it changes the wobble? What cork position makes your Wandersnatch jump the most? What makes it glide the smoothest? What makes it not move at all?

3

THE SALTY KINGDOM

ALL ABOARD, YE SCRAPPY SEA PONIES!

There be monsters lurking about! Luckily, these monsters don't bite. Well, except for that **Big Bite Bella** (page 70). The name really gives her away. Oh, and the **Bright-Light Pooferfins** (page 62) might bite, but that's more of an annoying nibble. Come to think of it, the **Magnetic Bumblebopper** (page 56) would bite if you got too close, and I don't know where a **Motorized Spongywhatsit's** (page 67) mouth even is. Okay, so maybe they all bite. Just keep your hands in the boat!

MAGNETIC BUMBLEBOPPER

Ahhhhhh, paradise! Nothing like being the only ones on an abandoned desert island. Just us, the tree, the flowers, and the waves. What's that you say, human friend? Oh yes, I hear that buzz that sounds like a giant bouncing bee-like monster too. It's probably just a motorboat or something. Pass me the bug spray, just in case.

FAST FACTS

WHAT: a magnetic creature that moves like a jittery pendulum as it reacts to other magnets below

DRILL TIME: This project uses a power drill for the tree trunk. See page 58 for more on drilling. If you don't want to use a drill, you can use a lot of hot glue and a supporting wood bead to make an angled tree trunk instead. ■ **STEAM STUFF:** magnetism ■ **DIFFICULTY:** ★ ★ ■ **COST:** $

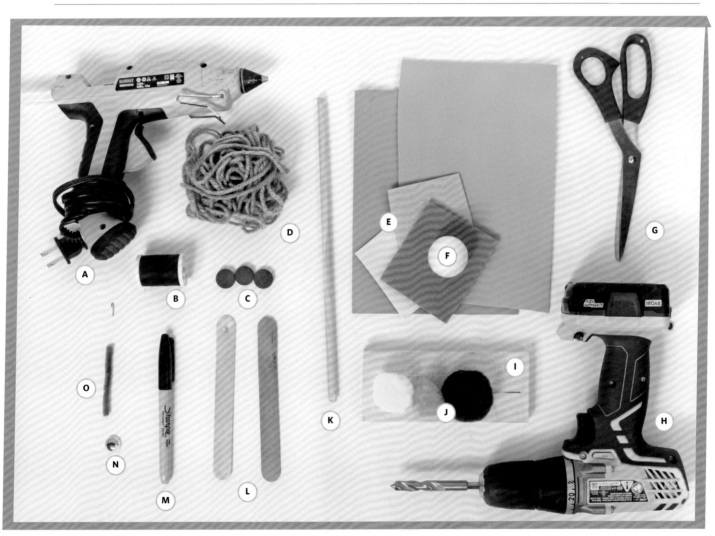

YOU WILL NEED

Ⓐ Hot glue gun   Ⓑ String   Ⓒ 3-4 magnets   Ⓓ Yarn   Ⓔ Craft foam   Ⓕ Styrofoam ball (can substitute other craft supply)

Ⓖ Scissors   Ⓗ Drill (with bit the width of your dowel)   Ⓘ Wood base   Ⓙ Pompoms   Ⓚ 1 dowel   Ⓛ 2 craft sticks

Ⓜ Marker   Ⓝ 1 googly eye   Ⓞ Metal wire (optional)

IT'S TIME TO DRILL!

Drills are great for making circular holes in things. But because they can be dangerous, your adult helper should be deciding whether they use the drill or whether you're ready to try. If you get to drill a hole, you'll want to know a couple things first. To make holes, you'll need *bits*, which are the long things that you screw into the end of drills. It's best to have a set with a couple of different sizes of bits. It's also great to have a surface that you can drill on that's okay to scratch up, because once you drill the hole you mean to drill, you don't want to accidentally drill a hole into your table. A scrap piece of wood works really well, and you can use it over and over again. When you drill, make sure to pay close attention. Use both hands, but keep your fingers away from the drilling.

1. **DRILL HOLE IN WOOD BASE.** Have your adult helper make the hole at an angle.

2. **PRESS AND GLUE DOWEL IN HOLE.** This will be the tree trunk.

3. **GLUE MAGNETS DOWN AS FLOWERS.** ❗ Save 1 magnet, but use the rest. Make sure all the magnets are oriented the same way by first stacking them so they sticking to one another. Now pull them apart and place them flat on the table, keeping the same sides up as when they were in the stack. Use glue gun to keep them in place near one another.

4. **WRAP THE TREE TRUNK IN YARN.**

5. **GLUE ON COCONUTS.** Add a couple of pompoms to the top of your tree for style.

6. **CUT AND GLUE ON TREETOP.** Use scissors and craft foam to design your own island tree.

CONTINUE ON TO PAGE 60

7. **MAKE FLOWER PETALS.** You can cut individual foam petals or rings to glue around the glued-down magnets.

8. **CREATE BUMBLEBOPPER WINGS.** Cut each of the craft sticks in half, and glue the halves to the sides of the Styrofoam ball. This will be the Bumblebopper.

9. **GIVE IT A FACE!** Every Bumblebopper has an attitude. What's your Bumblebopper's expression?

11. **HANG THE BUMBLEBOPPER ABOVE THE FLOWERS.** Use string to hang the Bumblebopper from the tree at a length that puts it pretty close to the flowers.

10. **GLUE A MAGNET TO THE BOTTOM OF THE BUMBLEBOPPER.** ❗ Take your 1 saved magnet and hold it above the others. Which way do you have to hold it so it pushes away from the others? Keep it facing that way as you glue it to the bottom of your Bumblebopper. This will make it jitter when it flies.

12. WATCH THAT BUMBLEBOPPER DANCE! Give it a nudge and watch it jiggle! Do you see it bouncing and spinning around? Why does it do that? Nudge it again and see if it does the same thing. If you're not getting a lot of wiggling, try lowering the string so the Bumblebopper is closer to the flowers.

STEAM STUFF
MAGNETIC PERSONALITY

That Bumblebopper sure does seem to work hard—but what keeps it going? If you pull it back and let it go, you'll find that it takes a wild path as it goes wiggling back and forth through the air over the flowers. This is because of the big weight it has glued to its bottom: the magnet! When two magnets attract, it's said that one's "north pole" is attracted to the other's "south pole." But can you make two magnets push away from each other? Try it with two magnets. See what happens when you flip one over. What happens when you flip both over? If you want to see the Bumblebopper take a different path, try peeling up a magnet and flipping it over before you glue it back down. What happens to the bug's bop?

EXPLORE SOME MORE

After watching a Bumblebopper, you may think you've seen it all. But what if it could do more? Try changing things like the string length, where the magnets are placed, how many magnets are stacked, and which side of the magnet is facing up to get some really weird results.

B..IG T-LIG. T P..OFERFINS

When the sun gets too hot, it's nice to dive down deep in our submarine. And to answer your question, yes, we have a submarine. Anyway, it can be hard to see in the ocean, but trust me, there are creatures lurking everywhere. Oh, look! It's a school of Bright-Light Pooferfins. I love these little puffballs. They may look like marshmallows, but they're the flashlights of the sea.

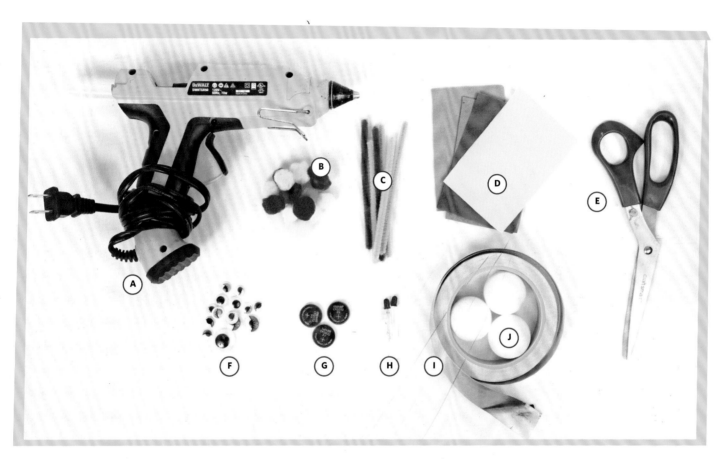

YOU WILL NEED

Ⓐ Glue gun   Ⓑ Pompoms and markers   Ⓒ Pipe cleaners   Ⓓ Small bits of craft foam   Ⓔ Scissors

Ⓕ Googly eye   Ⓖ 1 3-volt button cell (flat) battery   Ⓗ 1–2 LED lights   Ⓘ 1 roll copper tape   Ⓙ 1 styrofoam ball

MAKE YOUR MONSTER

1. **PLACE REAR BATTERY FIN.** Let's get poofing! Use scissors to make a notch in the Styrofoam ball for your battery, and push the battery in.

2. **APPLY 2 PIECES OF COPPER TAPE.** ❗ Cut 2 thin pieces of copper tape, remove the backing, and stick the pieces next to each other (but not touching!) on top of the Pooferfin's head. One piece of tape should be attached to one side of the battery, and the other piece attached to the other side.

3. **ADD FOAM FINS.** Let's add some finny flair! Cut out side fins and a head fin to give your Pooferfin its personality and something to swim with.

4. **GLUE ON EYES.** Every Pooferfin needs a face. You can add pompoms, use googly eyes, or even just draw on your face.

5. **TEST YOUR LED.** Spread the 2 legs of an LED light so that 1 leg touches 1 piece of tape, and the other leg touches the other piece of tape. Does it light up? If not, try switching the legs or checking the tape connections to the battery.

6. **DECORATE.** Add scales or other designs to your Pooferfin to make it unique.

7. **LIGHT UP THE NIGHT!** Push your LED light into the Styrofoam, and tape it if necessary to keep your light on. Try turning off the room lights to see the Pooferfins as if they were in their natural deep-water element.

STEAM STUFF

MOVING ELECTRICITY

What makes your Pooferfin light up? Just like with Reddi and Yullo, Pooferfins work by completing an electrical circuit. The two pieces of copper tape act like wires to bring electricity out to the top of the Pooferfin's head. When you bridge the two pieces of tape with an LED light, it lights up as if the legs were touching the battery directly. That's because the copper tape is a good *conductor* of electricity, meaning a thing that lets electricity move through it easily. Can you find other conductors around the house? Try using them to make an LED circuit with your battery.

TRY IT!

If you want to make your Pooferfin even brighter, try adding more LED lights to the top of its head. Can you make two light up? What about three, four, or even more?

MOTORIZED SPONGYWHATSIT

Sometimes you have to wait your whole life to see a mythical creature. I mean, we get to see monsters like Bigfoot and the Loch Ness Monster all the time for picnics, but we've never seen a *human* like you before. And we've never seen a Spongywhatsit either. Legends say they have motor tails, big floppy hands, and a love for donuts. Wait! There's one now!

FAST FACTS

WHAT: a propeller-driven motorboat made from a sponge, craft materials, and electronics
STEAM STUFF: propulsion, buoyancy ▪ **IN THE TUB:** This project requires water, and lots of it. Try this out in a tub, a pool, a bath, or even the open ocean. If the electronics ever stop working, don't worry. Dry them out and try again. ▪ **DIFFICULTY:** ★ ★ ▪ **COST:** $ $ $

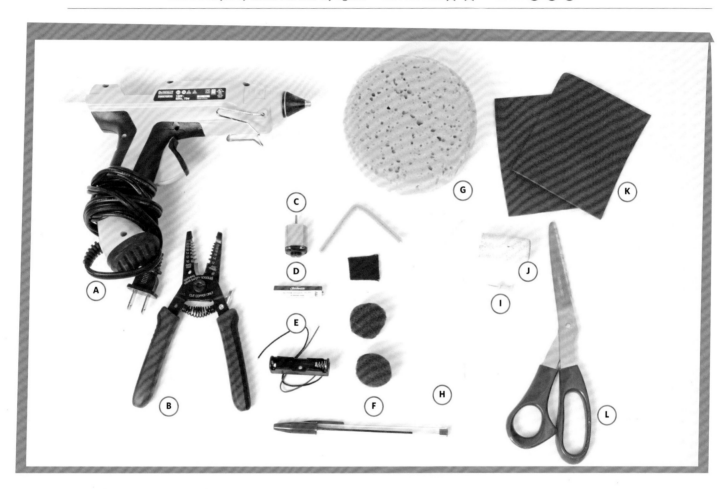

YOU WILL NEED

Ⓐ Glue gun Ⓑ Wire cutter Ⓒ 1 DC motor Ⓓ 1 AAA battery Ⓔ 1 AAA battery pack Ⓖ 1 large sponge

Ⓚ Scraps of craft foam Ⓗ 1 piece firm plastic (such as from a plastic bottle) Ⓕ Craft supplies for face

Ⓙ 1 cork Ⓘ 1 thumbtack Ⓛ Scissors

1. **GLUE MOTOR ON SPONGE.** Cut a notch in your sponge, and glue in your motor so the spinning end sticks out the back.

2. **CONNECT AND GLUE BATTERY PACK.** Trim the wires as needed and connect them to your motor by poking them through the motor's small metal tabs. Bend them over when they're in place. When you like the position, glue the battery pack to your sponge.

3. **BUILD A PROPELLER.** ❗ Cut a piece of cork and fasten it to a long skinny rectangle of plastic with a thumbtack. Fold the fins in opposite directions so your propeller can push water backward. This part requires experimenting, so try it out!

4. **PUSH PROPELLER ON MOTOR.** Push the center of the cork onto the spinning part of your motor.

5. **MAKE HANDS.** Cut some silly hands from craft foam and glue them on the sides of the sponge.

6. **PASTE ON A FACE.** Make it unique! Is your Spongywhatsit scary or kind?

7. TAKE IT ON THE HIGH SEAS!
Place in a battery to get your propeller spinning, and place the Spongywhatsit in a tub of water. Watch it whir and bump and spin! Which direction is it headed? Or is it headed in every direction?

STEAM STUFF
GOING PLACES

How does your Spongywhatsit know where to go? You can probably see that it doesn't know anything, really. However, a big thing that changes which direction it goes is the shape of the propeller. When the propeller spins in the tub, it pushes water in one direction, and the Spongywhatsit goes in the opposite direction. It's just like when you swim: you push water back with your hands, and your body moves forward. If you change the shape of the propeller, your Spongywhatsit will move differently. Give it a try! And next time you see a boat or airplane propeller, check out its shape for ideas.

EXPLORE SOME MORE

Can you control where your Spongywhatsit goes? After all, you're the captain. Try playing around with the motor and propeller to see what paths your creature takes. Can you make it go in a circle? What about a straight line? Can you make it veer to one side, go faster, or go slower? What affects it, and what else can you change?

BIG BITE BELLA

Have you met our pet, Bella? She's like an alligator crossed with a dog. Just throw a sailboat into the water, and she'll fetch it right out for you. Oh look, here she comes now. Here, girl! Who's our little cuddle monster? You can pet her if you want—she's very sweet. No, don't pet her near the teeth! Sorry, we're still training her not to nibble on humans.

FAST FACTS

WHAT: a wooden creature with a giant moveable mouth ▪ **STEAM STUFF:** mechanical motion
DRILL TIME: Big Bite Bella needs some drill work. See page 72 for more on drilling.
DIFFICULTY: ★ ★ ★ ▪ **COST:** $ $

YOU WILL NEED

(A) Glue gun   (B) 4 brad fasteners   (C) 2 long wooden sticks (paint stirrers work well)

(D) Paint and paintbrush   (E) Craft supplies for face   (F) 2 plastic syringes (without needles!)*

(G) Medum-size sheets of craft foam   (H) Scissors   (I) 1 piece of plastic tubing that fits syringe snugly**

(J) 7 wide craft sticks   (K) Markers   (L) Drill (with thin drill bit), and an adult helper to use it

*These syringes should be available at a store with a pharmacy, or they can be ordered online.
**Have your adult pick this up wherever they buy the syringes.

IT'S TIME TO DRILL!

Drills are great for making circular holes in things. But because they can be dangerous, your adult helper should be deciding whether they use the drill or whether you're ready to try. If you get to drill a hole, you'll want to know a couple things first. To make holes, you'll need *bits*, which are the long things that you screw into the end of drills. It's best to have a set with a couple of different sizes of bits. It's also great to have a surface that you can drill on that's okay to scratch up, because once you drill the hole you mean to drill, you don't want to accidentally drill a hole into your table. A scrap piece of wood works really well, and you can use it over and over again. When you drill, make sure to pay close attention. Use both hands, but keep your fingers away from the drilling.

1. **ASSEMBLE THE BODY.** Glue the 2 long sticks together with some overlap, and have your adult helper drill a hole near the end of one.

2. **ATTACH SYRINGES AND TUBE.** Glue 1 syringe near the undrilled end of the sticks, and the other syringe where the 2 sticks meet. Cut a tube to a length that can connect the 2 syringes.

3. **PAINT BODY.** Throw a nice shimmery coat of paint on your monster and let dry.

4. **DRILL AND ASSEMBLE STICKS FOR MOUTH.** ❗ Using 6 of the craft sticks, glue 2 sets of 2 sticks each together, (long jaw pieces) and set aside 2 sticks (short mouth pieces). Have your adult helper drill thin holes in the craft sticks as in the photo. They'll want to drill slowly. And if a craft stick breaks, you can always grab another.

5. **MAKE AND GLUE MOUTH ATTACHMENT.** With the 7th craft stick, cut out 2 pieces: a small wood square and the craft stick tip. Have your adult helper drill a hole in the tip piece, and glue it to the syringe as in the photo.

6. ATTACH LONG JAW PIECES. Use a brad fastener to go through the holes at the end of the long jaw pieces, and the hole on the mouth attachment. Spread the brad legs out to keep the craft sticks sandwiched together.

7. ATTACH SHORT MOUTH PIECES. Use brads to attach the shorter mouth pieces so that one end is attached to the hole in the big stick and the other ends are connecting to the long mouth pieces.

8. ADD SCALES. Give Bella some body by cutting out scales from craft foam. Glue them along the body and mouth, and draw on designs.

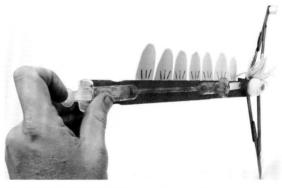

10. CHOMP AWAY, BELLA! Use the plunger of the syringe on the end to make Bella open and close her mouth. *Nom nom nom!* If Bella doesn't move at first, try looking around for the problem. You'll get those chompers moving!

9. MAKE A FACE. Design a face for your new friend from the deep. You can glue an eyeball on the central brad, and anything else you like, such as teeth, nostrils, or even a beard. Get creative!

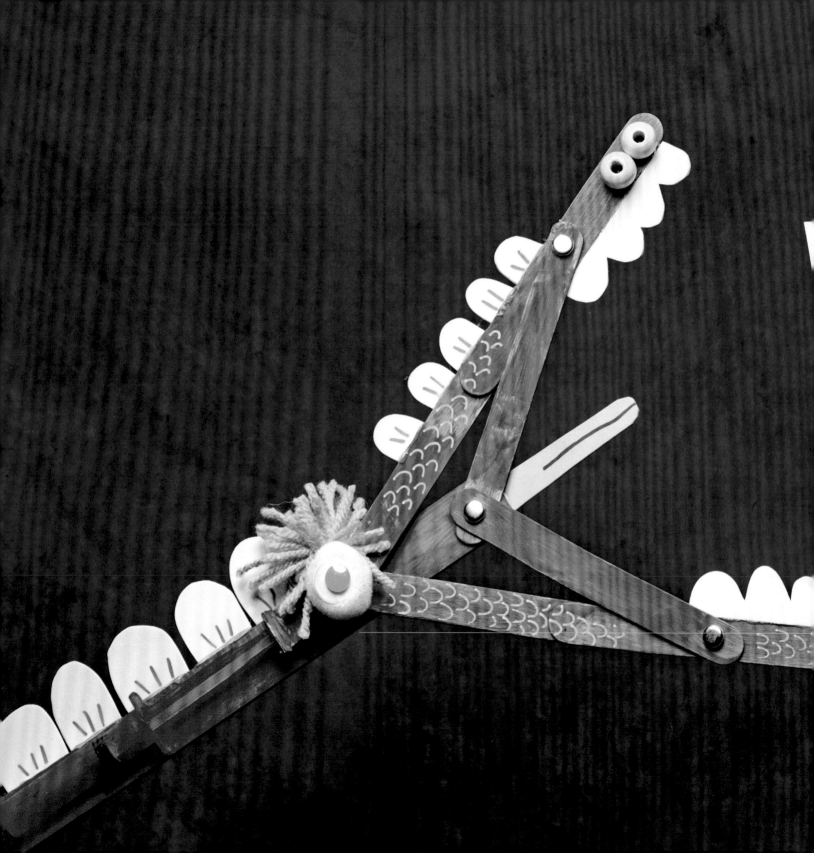

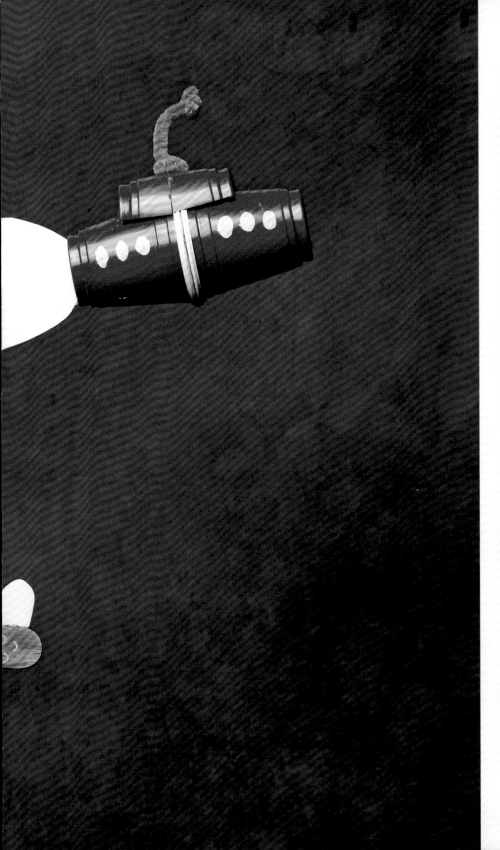

STEAM STUFF
MECHANICAL MOTION

What makes Bella bite? When you push the plunger of the syringe, it sets off a whole chain of mechanical motion. In this case, the word *mechanical* means "like a machine." Somehow, the motion of you pushing on the plunger transforms into Bella biting. How does this happen? See if you can trace the motion through the machine you just created. When you push the plunger, what happens next? And after that?

TRY IT!

When you push on the plunger, it may take a moment for Bella to move. Try filling both syringes and the tube with water and see what happens when you push down on the syringe. What's different?

EXPLORE SOME MORE

Bella's just one creature from the deep. There are a whole lot more you can make. Try changing the sizes and connections of the mouth to see what other big chompers are possible. Can you make a larger mouth? Or a mouth that isn't the same on both sides? Try making a more complicated Bella with an even bigger bite!

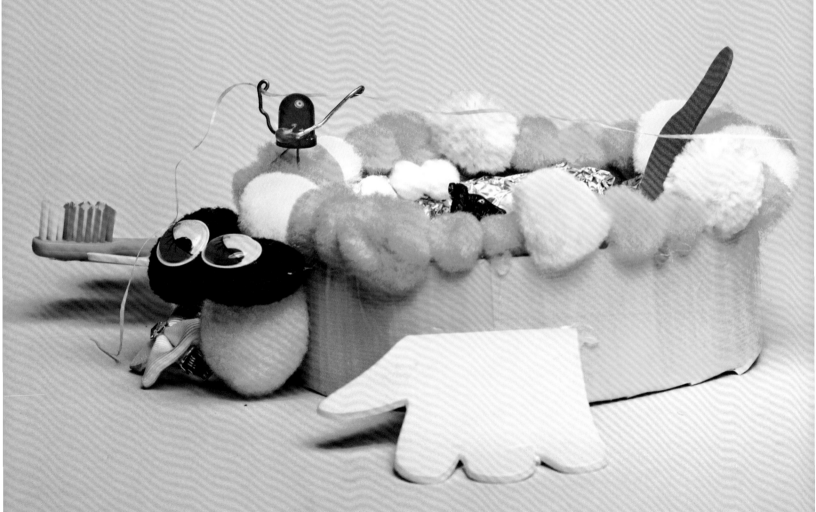

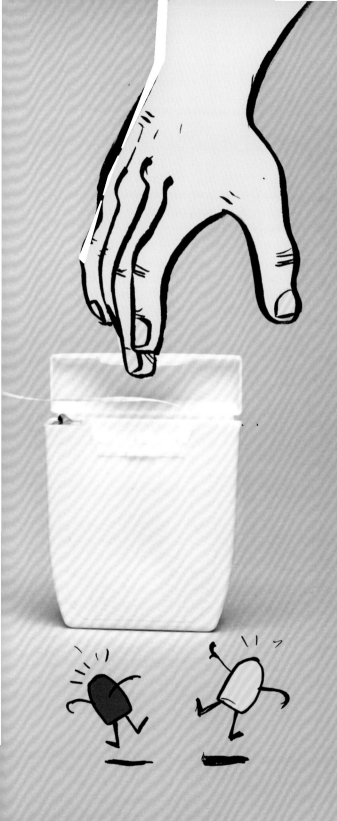

4

THE GIANT'S MEDIUM-SIZED HOTEL

BE QUIET CLIMBING UP THAT BEANSTALK!

At The Giant's Medium-Sized Hotel, we serve our guests from a safe distance with **The Giant's Food Flinger** (page 78). We have the finest sculptures on display straight from the artist's nose: **The Great Goblin's Boogers** (page 82). If you get a chance to visit the spa, we take care of our guests with **The Troll's Handsome Hands** (page 90) treatment. We also offer free mouth cleanings to our somewhat stinky-breathed guests with **The Ogre Dentist Service** (page 86). Trust me, it's mostly for our own good. Oh, I just heard an order come in to the restaurant. We better get that food flinger ready!

THE GIANT'S FOOD FLINGER

How do humans feed themselves again? You use forks and spoons and stuff, right? Yes, well, when feeding a giant, you'll definitely want to use a flinger. Whether you're serving up goblin tacos or salted elves, it's best to stay as far away as possible from the giant's mouth. Luckily, giants also really love eating pompoms. It's like candy for them. Fire up another one!

WHAT: a rubber-band-powered spoon catapult game ▪ **STEAM STUFF:** levers
DIFFICULTY: ★ ★ ▪ **COST:** $

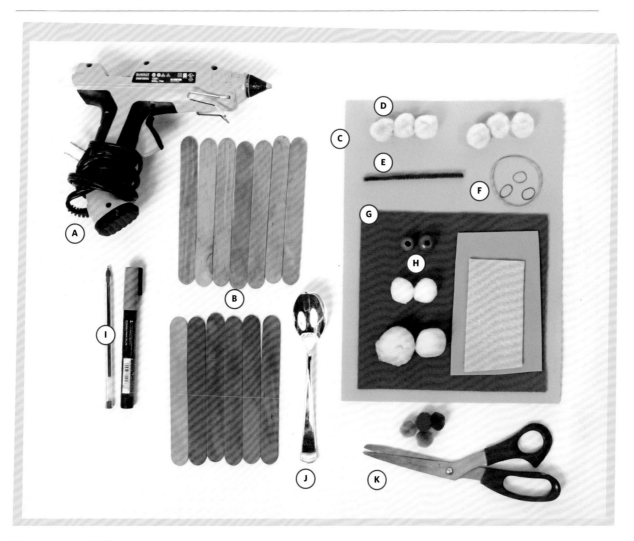

YOU WILL NEED

A Glue gun   B 13 wide craft sticks   C 1 large piece craft foam   D A few pompoms   E A few pipe cleaners

F 4 rubber bands   G 1 medium-size rectangle of felt   H A few wooden beads   I Markers   J 1 plastic spoon

K Scissors

1. **ASSEMBLE A CRAFT STICK STRUCTURE WITH 7 CRAFT STICKS.** ❗ Glue together a frame to mount your hungry giant on. Make a tilted table, with 2 of the legs shorter than the others. You'll need to cut 1 of the craft sticks to make the 2 shorter legs.

2. **GLUE ON POMPOM TEETH.** Use 2 pompoms to make a pair of pearly whites.

3. **ADD A FELT POMPOM CATCHER.** Glue rectangle of felt loosely within the craft stick frame.

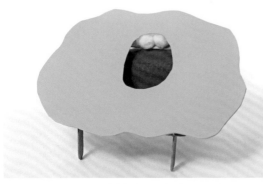

4. **CUT AND GLUE A FOAM HEAD.** The head can be any shape you want, but make a large mouth so the giant can catch its food easily. Use hot glue to attach the head to the craft stick frame.

5. **MAKE A GIANT FACE!** Give it some bead eyes, draw on some freckles, add a pipe cleaner mustache, and decorate with anything else you think your giant needs.

6. **LAUNCHER TIME!** Make a stack of 5 craft sticks. Use 2 rubber bands to hold the stack together.

7. **ATTACH BASE STICK AND PLASTIC SPOON.** Use a rubber band to hold the end of the spoon's handle and the end of the remaining craft stick together. Wedge the stack of craft sticks between the spoon handle and the single craft stick. Now you've got a food flinger!

8. **FEED THE HUNGRY GIANT!** Place a pompom in the bowl of the spoon, pull back the spoon, and let it go! Is your food-flinging accurate, or is it more of a pompom food fight?

STEAM STUFF
LOVER OF LEVERS

What do a seesaw, your arm, and the flood flinger have in common? They're all long things that are attached to other things. The seesaw is attached in the middle to the ground, your arm is fixed to your shoulder, and the food flinger is attached to a stack of craft sticks. We call the long part a *lever*, and we call what it's attached to a *fulcrum*. Levers help give power, especially when flinging things. In the case of the food flinger, the plastic spoon is our lever, and the stack of craft sticks is our fulcrum. Try looking around for other levers and fulcrums in your surroundings. What can you find? You might want to search quickly if there's a hungry giant nearby.

TRY IT!

Try moving the craft stick stack relative to the spoon. What happens if you move it forward or backward? Which flinger design shoots the farthest? Which shoots the highest? How else could you redesign your food flinger to shoot pompoms from even farther away? After all, you can never be too far from a giant.

THE GREAT GOBLIN'S BOOGERS

Bravo! Bravo! The sign says these sculptures are some of the Great Goblin's artistic masterpieces. Each one is unique, magnificent, and carefully crafted by the goblin's . . . let me read the sign here . . . nose? Wait a minute. These are all boogers?! Whenever we blow our noses, mom makes us throw away the tissues. We would've become famous artists!

WHAT: strange balanced sculptures made of melted and resolidified wax crayons

STEAM STUFF: rock cycle ■ **HOT STUFF:** This project uses a stove and involves very hot water. Use caution, because boogers are fun, but burns are not. This is a great time to use an adult helper. After all, adults like to make amazing art too. ■ **DIFFICULTY:** ★ ★ ■ **COST:** $ $

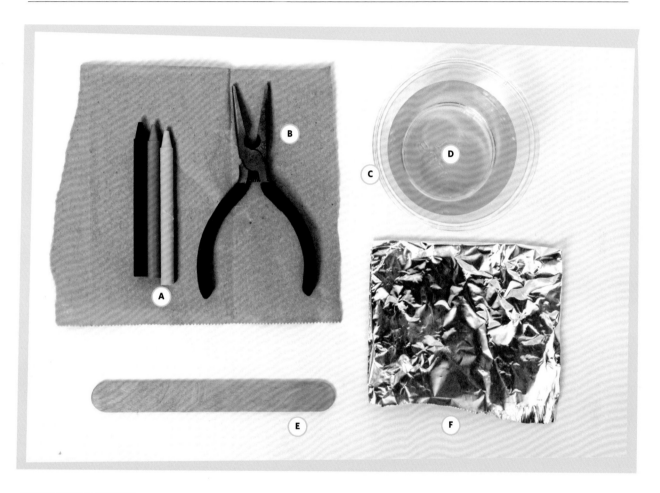

YOU WILL NEED

Ⓐ Several crayons   Ⓑ Pliers or tongs   Ⓒ 1 clear cup   Ⓓ Water   Ⓔ 1 craft stick   Ⓕ Medium-size sheet of aluminum foil   ● Cooking pot   ● Hot plate or stove

MAKE YOUR MONSTER

1. **BREAK UP 2 CRAYONS.** Remove the paper labels, and break up the crayon wax into tiny pieces using your hands and a craft stick.

2. **MAKE A FOIL BOAT.** Tear off a bit of foil, and fold it into a watertight boat about 3 inches long. Give your boat a flat bottom and tall sides.

3. **POUR CRAYON CHUNKS INTO BOAT.**

4. **HEAT UP WATER.** Use caution and an adult helper. You can heat up water in a cooking pot on a hot plate or on the stove, so long as it's easy to access the water's surface. You want your water hot but not boiling.

5. **PLACE FOIL BOAT IN HOT WATER.** Use pliers or tongs, depending on what is safe and comfortable for the situation.

6. **ONCE THE CRAYONS ARE MELTED, POUR LIQUID WAX INTO CUP OF COLD WATER.**
   ❗ This takes practice! Remove your boat from the water with a tongs or pliers. Pour the boat's liquid wax into the water from a couple of inches above, and all at once. As the wax enters the water, it immediately "freezes." Each shape turns out different!

STEAM STUFF
LAVA

Some have compared the goblin's nose to a volcano, but for more reasons than you might think. When you make goblin boogers, you are actually going through the same process that happens when rocks form on Earth. When you break up the crayons with a craft stick, this is similar to the erosion and *sedimentary* process that rocks go through, getting broken down and mixed up. When you heat up the crayon bits, the wax passes through the *metamorphic* stage, and then becomes liquid just like *igneous* lava. When the wax cools down, it becomes solid again and takes on a new form. If you look closely, you can see ridges, bubbles, and other shapes that look a lot like freshly cooled lava. Check out photos of new lava rock to compare! And have fun creating brand new lava boogers.

TRY IT!

A master sculptor is always trying new techniques. Try melting more than two crayons, adjusting the cup's water temperature, and changing the height you pour the wax from, for starters.

7. **GAZE UPON YOUR MASTERPIECE!** Bravo! Bravo! The public is awaiting your next piece! If you don't like your artwork, dry it off and melt it down to start over.

You might find anything in an ogre's mouth. We've found couches and baseball bats, and once Reddi found a telephone pole that had been used as a toothpick. Reddi always says that it's better to be taking stuff out of an ogre's mouth than to be put in. Of course, they might roar a little bit when you poke them, but I think that's just ogre speak for "thank you." Now, let's see what we can take out of there . . .

YOU WILL NEED

(A) Glue gun   (B) 1 roll colorful duct tape   (C) 1 large piece cardboard   (D) 1 large piece aluminum foil
(E) A few medium-size sheets craft foam   (F) 2 googly eyes   (G) Several small objects to put in ogre mouth
(H) 1 pair metal tweezers   (I) 1 AAA battery and single battery pack   (J) 1 1.5-volt to 3-volt buzzer   (K) 1 small roll
insulated electrical wire   (L) 1 roll electrical tape   (M) Lots of pompoms   (N) Scissors   (O) Pen   (P) Wire strippers

1. **CUT AND GLUE A CARDBOARD BASE.** Cut a cardboard circle or oval, and then glue on a thin cardboard strip as a wall along its edge.

2. **ADD DUCT TAPE AND FOIL.** Tape the outside of the cardboard for color, and foil the inside as part of the circuit.

3. **CONNECT 1 OF THE BUZZER WIRES TO A BATTERY PACK WIRE.** Strip the ends of all the wires so that there is some metal wire exposed. Put a battery in the pack, and see if you can make the buzzer go by connecting both wires. You may have to switch which wires are connected to make a sound. When you find the right orientation, twist 1 of the battery wires with the buzzer wire that it's connected to. Press on some aluminum foil to make a good connection, and then add some electrical tape to seal it off.

4. **CONNECT THE OTHER BUZZER WIRE TO THE METAL TWEEZERS.** ❗ Cut an extra piece of electrical wire and strip both ends, exposing the metal underneath. Connect 1 end of the wire to the available end of the buzzer wire, and the other end to the tweezers. Use foil on both connections, and seal them up with electrical tape.

5. **CONNECT THE OPEN BATTERY WIRE TO THE FOIL LINING THE OGRE'S CARDBOARD MOUTH.** Press a wad of foil around the exposed end of the battery wire. Tape it to the foil in the ogre's mouth.

6. **TEST YOUR CIRCUIT!** Try touching the tweezers to the foil in the ogre's mouth. Did it set off the buzzer? If it doesn't work, play with all the connections. It's okay if this takes some time to troubleshoot! Your ogre can wait.

7. **GLUE BUZZER AND BATTERY PACK TO WALL AROUND OGRE'S MOUTH.** Make some hands. Cut some foam hands and glue them to the cardboard wall.

8. **MAKE SOME HANDS.** Cut some foam hands and glue them to the cardboard wall.

9. **ADD SOME EYES.** Use pompoms with googly eyes and anything else to give your ogre a special look.

10. **DECORATE!** You can add a tongue, pompoms along the rim, teeth, and anything else you want! Give your ogre some style.

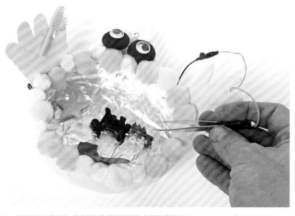

11. **OPEN YOUR OGRE DENTIST OFFICE!** Place some objects in the ogre's mouth, and challenge your friends to see if they can use the tweezers to take out the objects without making the ogre buzz!

STEAM STUFF
DRAWING CIRCUITS

You just made a pretty impressive circuit! You have a battery, a buzzer, tweezers, and some foil. When people make circuits this big, they often draw an illustration of all the parts to keep track of it. Can do you draw a picture of the electrical parts of your ogre? Try drawing and labeling the parts and then draw all the connections. These drawings are called *circuit diagrams*. They help others see how you put something together.

TRY IT!

You can use your ogre to play a game. Place a bunch of objects in the ogre's mouth. Take turns with friends, having each person try to take out one object at a time. If the ogre buzzes, the object goes back in, and the tweezers go to the next person. If the ogre doesn't buzz, keep the object and hand the tweezers to the next person. Whoever ends up with the most objects at the end wins! You can also play by points, assigning different points for easier or more difficult objects.

THE TROLL'S ANDSOME ANDS

Trolls are some of the hardest working monsters in all of monster kingdom. They might spend the morning ripping off roofs, an afternoon tossing cars, and an evening tearing up trees and crushing buildings. Our troll friends tell us it's exhausting! We like to help them take care of their hardworking hands. You know, a troll may do bad things, but they should get to look great while they do it. Care to work on one with us, human friend?

FAST FACTS

WHAT: a wearable arm with controllable, moving fingers
STEAM STUFF: anatomy ▪ **DIFFICULTY:** ★ ★ ★ ▪ **COST:** $

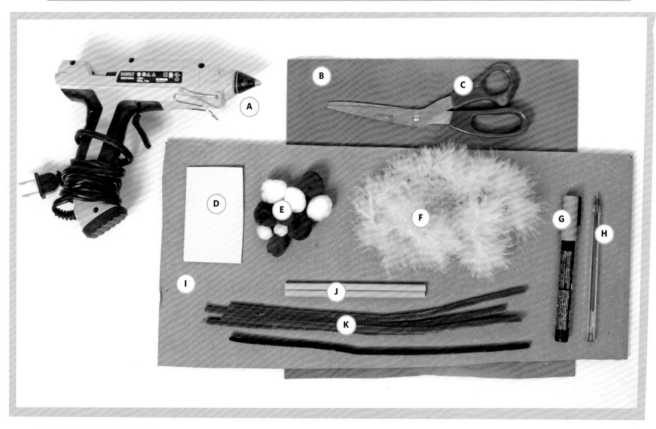

YOU WILL NEED

Ⓐ Glue gun   Ⓑ 1 large piece craft foam   Ⓒ Scissors   Ⓓ Small piece of craft foam   Ⓔ Several pompoms
Ⓕ 1 feather boa   Ⓖ Colorful markers   Ⓗ Pen   Ⓘ 1 large piece cardboard   Ⓙ 2 straws   Ⓚ 4 pipe cleaners
Ⓛ 2 wide craft sticks

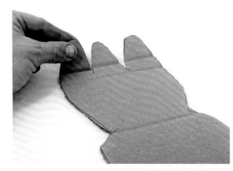

1. **DRAW AND CUT A HANDSOME HAND OUTLINE ON YOUR CARDBOARD.** Make a hand and arm large enough to slide over your own hand and forearm. Make sure to cut wide, separated fingers.

2. **CREASE KNUCKLES AND WRIST.** Bend fingers and wrist back and forth a few times to make your troll's hand joints. If you're wondering where to bend the cardboard, just look at your own fingers and wrist for reference.

3. **CUT 12 SMALL STRAW PIECES.** Make each about ½ inch long.

5. **INSERT PIPE CLEANERS THROUGH STRAW PIECES.** Hook each pipe cleaner around the straw near the fingertip, and add a dab of hot glue. Thread the pipe cleaner through the other straws on each finger. At the other end of the pipe cleaner, make a loop.

4. **GLUE STRAW PIECES ALONG FINGERS AND HAND.** Place 1 straw piece in the space between the joints (folds). These straw pieces will act as the troll's hand bones.

6. **TEST FINGER ACTION.** Pull back and forth on each loop to watch each finger bend!

7. **MAKE WRIST HOLDER.** Make 2 holes in the corners of the cardboard at the end of the arm, and loop a pipe cleaner through these holes. You can tighten or loosen the pipe cleaner to fit your arm.

8. **ADD CRAFT STICK SUPPORTS.** Glue 2 craft stick supports along the troll's arm to keep it rigid.

9. **CUT AND GLUE A COLORFUL FOAM LAYER.** Trace an outline of the cardboard hand on your craft foam. Cut it out, and glue the foam to the clean side of the cardboard.

10. **MAKE THE HAND HANDSOME.** Glue on pompoms, add some foam fingernails, and play around with hand designs using markers, pipe cleaners, and even a boa bracelet. It's manicure time!

11. **LEND YOURSELF A HAND!** Slide your arm through the wrist holder, and put your fingers in the loops. Practice bending the fingers and wrists, and then show off your Troll's Handsome Hand. Who knew you were part troll?

STEAM STUFF
WORKING HANDS

It may look a little different at first, but this troll's hand works very similarly to your own. The straws are like bones and the creases are like joints. But what are the pipe cleaners like? When you want to move your fingers, your brain makes your muscles pull on little ropes attached to your bones. These are called *tendons*, and you can feel them if you put a hand on the other wrist while you wiggle your other fingers. This combination of muscles, bones, joints, and tendons is what makes your hand work so well—and makes a troll's hand work even better.

TRY IT!

Trolls come in all shapes and sizes. Try making another hand with more joints, more fingers, or differently shaped hands. Using cardboard and pipe cleaners, you can even make hands that grab or pinch, instead of just curl. What designs can you come up with?

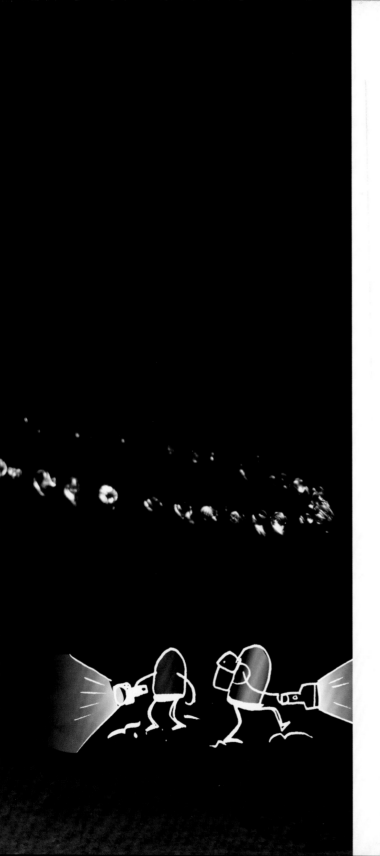

THE CAVES OF MAYBE NO RETURN

UMMM, REDDI? YOU BROUGHT THE MAP, RIGHT?

We're definitely not scared. We're so brave that—WHAT WAS THAT?! Oh, sorry, that was just Reddi. Whew! All right, we need a plan if we're going to make it through this spooky cavern. If I remember right, there are just a few monsters we need to watch out for. We'll have to stay out of reach of the **Haunted Hands of Hoogamagee** (page 96) and shield ourselves from the slobber of **Drools McGoo** (page 102) if we want to make it to **Fortoona the Truthteller** (page 106). From there, we'll just need to get past **Ol' Webby Bent Legs** (page 110). Then we're out! Easy peasy, right?

▮AUNTED ▮ANDS OF HOOGAMAGEE

Oh my. Did that hand just look at us? I didn't even know hands had eyes before coming down here. Human friend, these things look your size! Maybe if you make one, they'll seem less scary. But whatever you do, don't give it a high-five in the face.

FAST FACTS

WHAT: disposable glove creatures that self-inflate and launch with dry ice
STEAM STUFF: states of matter ▪ **DIFFICULTY:** ★ ▪ **COST:**

YOU WILL NEED

Ⓐ Glue gun   Ⓑ Craft supplies for decoration   Ⓒ Markers   Ⓓ 1 plastic cup   Ⓔ 1 chunk dry ice

Ⓕ 1 disposable glove (latex or nitrile)   Ⓖ A little water   Ⓗ Thick gloves (for handling dry ice)

DRY ICE ALERT! This project uses dry ice, which is a solid form of carbon dioxide. It can be tricky to find, but the effort is worth it. While it is supercool, it is also *supercold*. It is amazing to look at it, but it can hurt if you touch it directly, and it can be very harmful if swallowed or put in a closed container. Your adult helper will need to buy the dry ice and help you use it in this project. Don't worry, they will use thick gloves to stay safe.

1. **START WITH DECORATION.** Give your Haunted Hand of Hoogamagee the personality you know it has by drawing on it and gluing fun features to it.

2. **PLACE A SMALL CHUNK OF DRY ICE IN EMPTY CUP.** Caution! Make sure your adult helper is running the show on this step and wearing thick gloves.

4. **STRETCH GLOVE OVER CUP.** 🛈 As the dry ice and water begin to react with each other, stretch your glove over the cup so it completely seals off the opening.

5. **YOUR HAND OF HOOGAMAGEE IS ALIVE!** Watch as your hand grows and grows, and if you're lucky, eventually goes *poof* and flies up off the cup. If it flies off, just have your adult helper add more dry ice and start over!

3. **POUR A LITTLE WATER INTO THE CUP.** You don't need much.

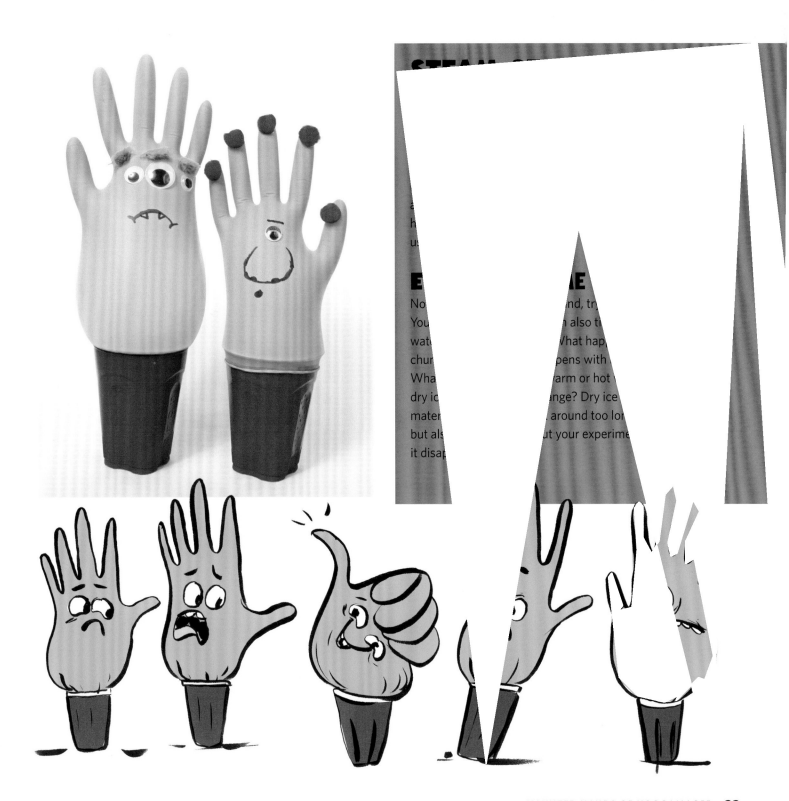

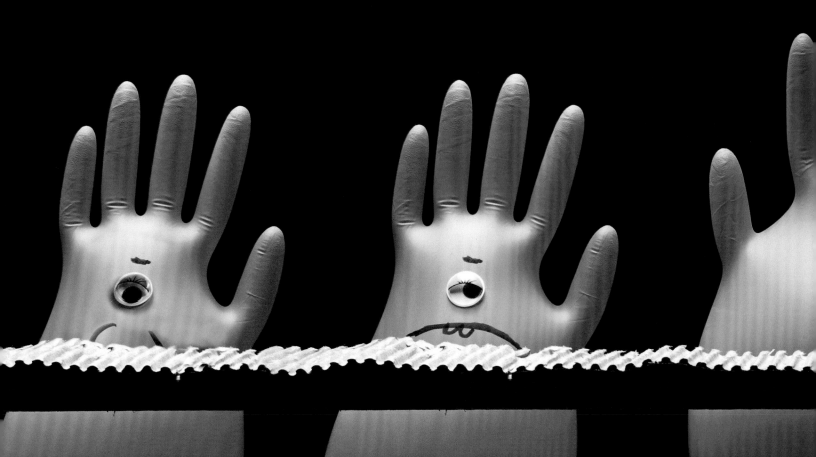

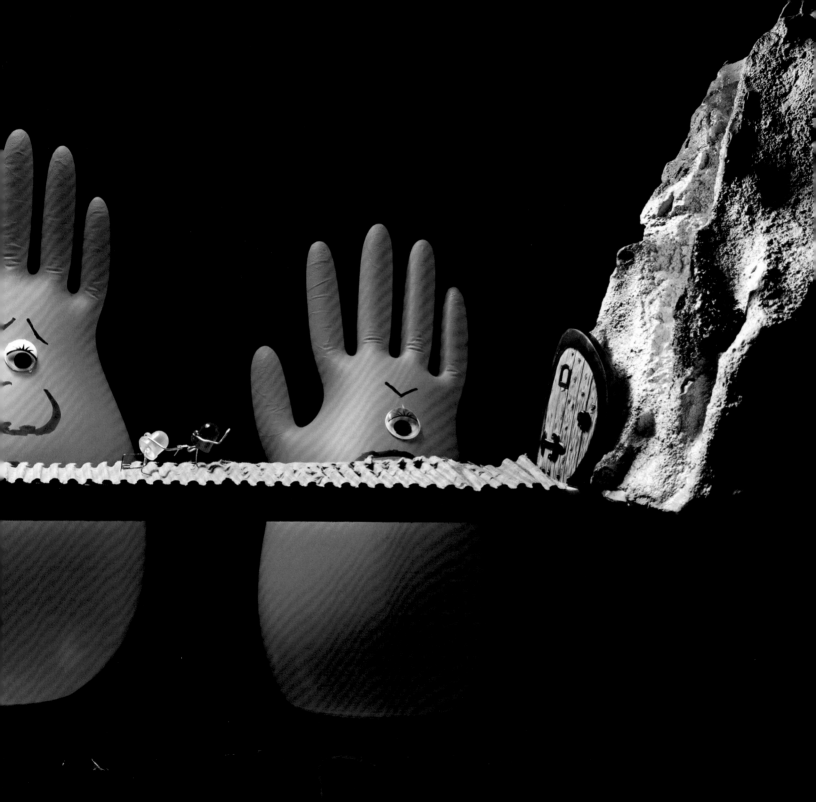

DROOLS McGOO

Put up the umbrellas and take out the ponchos! No, it's not rain exactly. It's Drools McGoo and wow, this monster can really slobber up a storm. I would say you should take cover, human friend. But with the way this thing spits, you should probably just take along a towel.

FAST FACTS

WHAT: a water sprinkler that sprays drops in circles when you give it a spin ▪ **STEAM STUFF:** centripetal force ▪ **TOO DROOL FOR COOL:** Drools McGoo spreads as much water as joy. Make sure you're in a place where it's okay to get your surroundings a little damp. ▪ **DIFFICULTY:** ★ ▪ **COST:** $

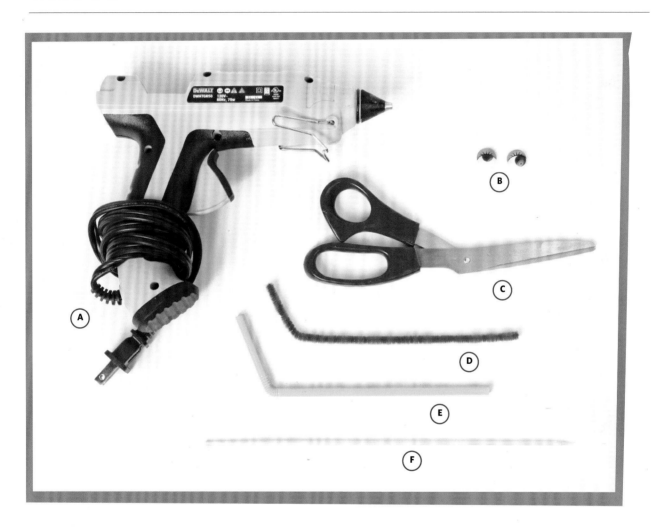

YOU WILL NEED

Ⓐ Glue gun Ⓑ 2 googly eyes Ⓒ Scissors Ⓓ 1 pipe cleaner Ⓔ 1 bendy straw Ⓕ 1 wood skewer

● 1 cup ● Some water

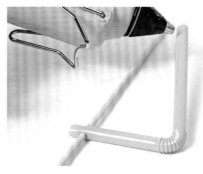

1. **TRIM BENDY STRAW.** Cut about 2 inches off the long end of the bendy straw to make Drools a little smaller.

2. **POKE HOLE IN STRAW WITH SKEWER.** Poke all the way through, near the short end of the bendy straw.

3. **GLUE FREE END OF STRAW TO SKEWER.** Add just a dot of glue to attach the bottom of the straw to the wood skewer. Leave the end of the straw open.

4. **CUT A MOUTH AT THE STRAW'S BEND.** Cut out a little bit of the straw right at the bend. This will be where Drools spits out water. You can experiment with changing the size and location of the mouth later.

5. **ADD EYES AND ARMS.** Bring Drools to life! Cut and bend pipe cleaner bits, and use some glue and googly eyes to give Drools a personality.

6. **GIVE DROOLS A SPIN!** Place Drools in a cup of water so the water level is higher than the bottom of the straw. Spin it around to watch Drools turn into a slobbery fountain.

STEAM STUFF
MOVING IN CIRCLES

So how does Drools McGoo spit, anyway? Well, have you ever held on to a friend's hands and spun in circles? You hold on tight, but it feels like if you let go, you'll both just fly apart. When things move in circles, they experience something called *centripetal force*, a force that pushes them away from the center of the circle. With your friend, the center is your hands in the middle. With Drools, it's the wooden skewer. As Drools spins, water enters into the bottom of the straw at the center of the circle and then gets pushed away from the center. The only direction is up the straw, where it eventually escapes out the mouth and flies everywhere. Try spinning Drools faster! What happens to the water coming out?

EXPLORE SOME MORE

Maybe you're ready to make Drools a bunch of brothers and sisters. Before you do, think about this: you can change things like the length of the straw, the size of the mouth, and even the number of straws on a single skewer! Experiment with other designs to see how they spit water differently.

FORTOONA THE TRUTHTELLER

Fortoona can answer all questions. Yessiree, the last time Reddi and I were here, we were just about to meet you. And we had *so many* questions about what you'd be like, human friend. We asked it all sorts of things like: Do humans have thick fur? How many tentacles does a human have? Will humans smell better or worse than Chompi? We fed Fortoona the questions, and the answers that popped out were mostly right. So go ahead and ask her a question. What do you wonder about?

YOU WILL NEED

(A) Glue gun   (B) 1 milk or juice carton   (C) A few pipe cleaners   (D) A few pieces of cardstock   (E) Scissors

(F) Lots of craft foam   (G) Markers   (H) 12 inches of boa or other hairy material   (I) 2 googly eyes   (J) Buttons

(K) Some pompoms   ● Tape

MAKE YOUR MONSTER

1. **CUT A WEDGE OUT OF THE CARTON.** Flip your milk carton upside down, and cut it off at an angle so Fortoona sits at an angle, facing a little toward the sky.

2. **CUT 2 RECTANGULAR HORIZONTAL SLOTS IN FRONT.** Cut a high slot and a low slot, both wide enough for your question cards to pass through. These will be the start and finish of Fortoona's ramps.

3. **CUT DOORS ON BACK.** Cut the back of the carton so that you can open it like 2 doors.

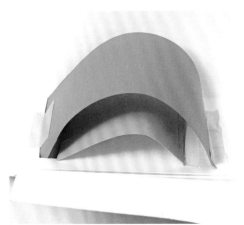

4. **CUT AND TAPE CARDSTOCK RAMPS.**
❗ Cut 2 rectangles of cardstock, one longer than the other. As in the photo, tape the shorter rectangle in a curve connecting the bottom of the upper slot with the top of the lower slot. Then tape the longer rectangle in a curve connecting the top of the upper slot with the bottom of the lower slot. This will make a double ramp, or tunnel, that connects Fortoona's mouth to its belly.

5. **CUT OUT AND WRITE QUESTION CARDS.** Use your imagination! You can ask questions about the future, write math problems, ask trivia questions, anything!

6. **WRITE ANSWERS ON BACKS OF CARD.** Shhhhh! This is the secret of Fortoona's magic. On the back of each card, write the answer to the question on its front. This way, when you feed Fortoona's mouth a question, the curved ramp can flip the card over and return it through Fortoona's belly with the answer facing up.

7. **GLUE ON SOME FOAM SKIN.** Cut a piece of foam the size of the carton's face, with rectangular holes to match the slots on the carton.

8. **MAKE A TRUSTWORTHY FACE.** Who wouldn't believe a face like Fortoona's? Glue on some googly eyes, hair, pompoms, and lips to give Fortoona a face that can tell the future and the past. You can also add buttons to Fortoona's shirt.

9. GIVE FORTOONA A HAND (OR TWO).
Cut out foam hands and pipe cleaner arms to give Fortoona posable hands to hold your question cards.

10. WITNESS FORTOONA'S INFINITE WISDOM!
Have Fortoona answer questions for all who seek them. Try feeding Fortoona questions, and see if friends or family can figure out what's going on!

STEAM STUFF
RAMPS

When you give Fortoona a question to digest, you're sending it down a ramp. This ramp (or double ramp) takes cards, flips them over, and sends them out below. Ramps can take on many shapes and can look like anything from a skate park halfpipe to a spiral slide to a roller coaster. We use ramps to help things move from place to place, and they are important in many parts of society. They're so important we've even named the ramp as one of the *six simple machines*, the basic building blocks of human engineering. So what ramps can you find in your world and what do they do?

TRY IT!

To really mix it up, you can turn Fortoona into a yes-or-no question answerer. Make a bunch of cards that are each blank on one side, and have an answer like "Yes," "No," "Maybe," "Try Again," and so forth written on the other side. Ask a question, pick a card, and feed Fortoona for your answer.

OL' WEBBY BENT LEGS

There are two things to know about Ol' Webby. The first thing is that the only way out of Ol' Webby's lair is to beat her in a game of cards. The second thing is that Ol' Webby hides an ace up all eight of her sleeves. I tried to call her out for cheating, once, but then Yullo reminded me that she's ten times bigger than we are and has pointy teeth. So, human friend. Can you give us a leg up? Or eight?

FAST FACTS

WHAT: a hydraulic-powered bendy spider that you can make do push-ups
STEAM STUFF: hydraulics ▪ **DIFFICULTY:** ★ ★ ★ ▪ **COST:** 💲 💲

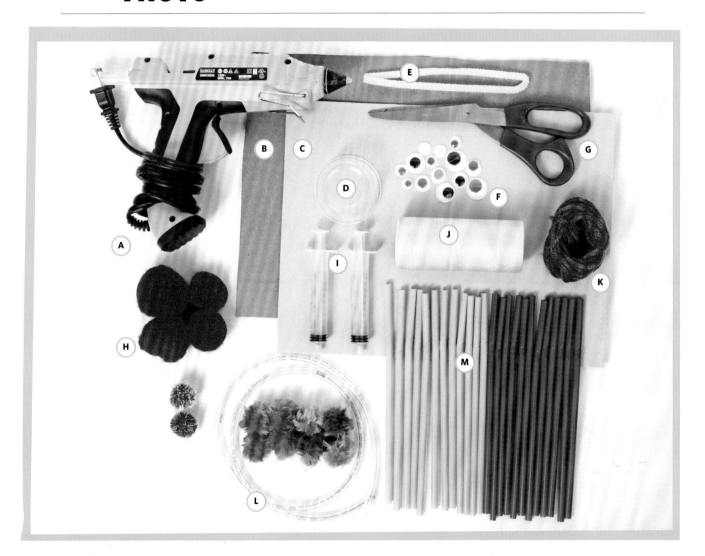

YOU WILL NEED

Ⓐ Glue gun   Ⓑ 1 cardboard sheet   Ⓒ Medium-size sheet of craft foam   Ⓓ 1 small cup   Ⓔ A few pipe cleaners

Ⓕ Lots of googly eyes   Ⓖ Scissors   Ⓗ Lots of pompoms   Ⓘ 2 plastic syringes (without needles!)*   Ⓙ 1 cardboard tube

Ⓚ Ball of yarn   Ⓛ 12 inches of plastic tubing that fits over syringe tip snugly**   Ⓜ Lots of bendy straws

*These syringes should be available at a store with a pharmacy, or they can be ordered online.
**Have your adult pick this up wherever they buy the syringes.

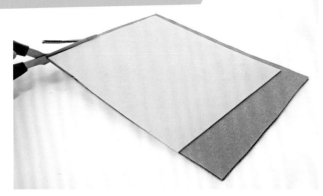

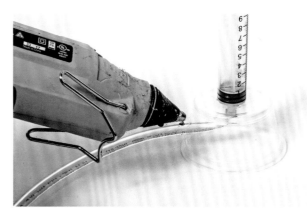

1. **MAKE A LARGE CARDBOARD PLATFORM.** You can glue on some craft foam for color.

2. **CREATE A SYRINGE BASE.** Cut a hole in the base and side of your plastic cup. Turn it upside and down, and fit the tip of the syringe through the hole in the base of the cup. Glue it in place so the syringe can stand upright. Run the tubing through the side hole of your plastic cup.

3. **GLUE CUP TO PLATFORM.** Ring the rim of your cup in hot glue, and hold it down in the middle of your cardboard

4. **ATTACH WEBBY'S BODY ON TOP OF SYRINGE.** Glue the cardboard tube on top of the plunger of the upright syringe, and wrap it in yarn.

5. **MAKE AN ALL-SEEING FACE.** Add some pompoms, lots of random eyes, and some antennae to give Webby some character.

6. **TRIM BENDY STRAWS.** Cut the bendy straws so they are about the same length on both sides of the bend.

7. **ASSEMBLE LEGS.** Fit 3 straws at a time into each other, end to end. Make as many of these 3-straw legs as you want!

8. **GLUE LEGS TO BODY AND PLATFORM.** Glue 1 end of each leg to Webby's body and the other to the platform. You can snip the leg's end to make a flatter gluing surface.

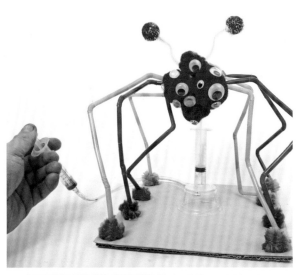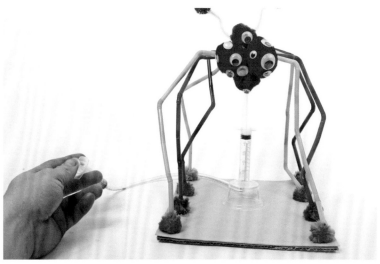

9. **CONNECT SECOND SYRINGE.** First pull the upright syringe so it is as tall as it can go. Push the plunger of the free syringe all the way in, and attach it to the other end of the tubing.

10. **MAKE WEBBY DO PUSH-UPS!** Get ready for some aerobics! Push and pull the second syringe to make Webby do a dance!

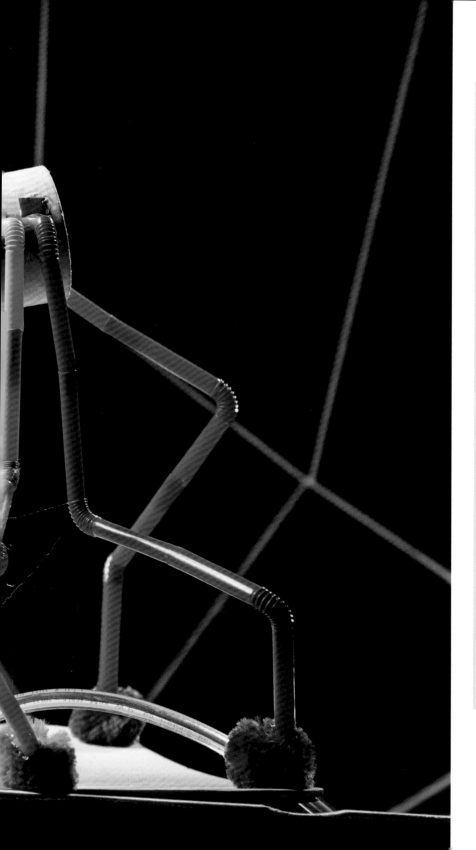

STEAM STUFF
HYDRAULICS

The syringes are like a remote control that doesn't need batteries. By hooking up Ol' Webby, you're able to push on one syringe, and have the other pop up. This type of machine is called a *hydraulic* or *pneumatic* machine, which means it uses air or water to help push things around. To hook it up, try pushing one plunger all the way down and pulling the other all the way up. Connect the two syringes with your plastic tubing, and push down on the "up" plunger. What happens to the other one? You can find machines like this all over the place, especially when they need lots of power. They're used for tools in construction like jackhammers and power drills, to make things pop out in haunted houses, and even to make cars jump up and down on the street. What examples of hydraulics can you find?

TRY IT!

If you want to make Ol' Webby spring up even faster, try filling the syringes and tube with water. Since water isn't as squishy as air, when you push the syringe down on one side, the other will spring up more quickly. You might get a little wet in the process, but give it a go!

WELL, LOOK AT YOU, HUMAN FRIEND!

You made it. And you made all those marvelous monsters along the way! We promise to tell your story for years to come, even if nobody believes us. Hope to see you down the road!

After all, you're pretty marvelous too.

ACKNOWLEDGMENTS

These monsters would still just be piles of straws and craft sticks if it weren't for the following helpful humans. Thank you to all of them for lending their wild talents and even wilder imaginations.

 To **Trevor Spencer**, master illustrator, for being able to wave his magic wand of a pen at a bunch of plastic straws and craft sticks and turn them into imaginative drawings on the page. Thank you for giving life to these humble creations.

 To **Young Xie**, supernatural designer, who could make even a jar of cat toenails look like the cutest thing you've ever seen in your whole life. Thank you for making these monsters look their sharpest.

 To **Jeffrey Schwinghammer**, omnipotent photographer, for playing wizard with lights and camera to open up a portal from our world to the monsters'. Thank you for making these projects sparkle.

Also a big thank you to the following folks, who helped in ways bigger than they knew. **Hannah Shulman**, infinitely patient enabler of crafting mayhem. **Thom O'Hearn**, best book coach in the biz. **Connor Schmidt**, set builder and hand model in a time of need. **Arvind Gupta**, inspiring friend and broadcaster of so many good ideas. **Dan Sudran** and the **Mission Science Workshop**, for giving me the place to learn as I taught.

INDEX

ABOUT THE AUTHOR

Sam Haynor loves things that go *whoosh*, *ping*, *doink*, and *bonk*! Sam has below-average crafting skills but an above-average love of pompoms. He graduated from some places and worked at others, and has been greatly inspired by his students and their incredible imaginations that never seem to stop inventing. While teaching, he became hooked on the idea that change in one's life can come from making things that are personally meaningful— or even making things from trash. He really likes trash. Come find him at the Exploratorium museum in San Francisco, where he currently works as an Exhibit Developer. He'll probably try to convince you to help him build something.

Sam is donating his proceeds from *Marvelous Makeable Monsters* to the nonprofit **Mission Science Workshop**, an incredible educational institution in San Francisco that empowers young explorers to ask why and then follow up on their questions. It also taught him to do the same.